# Hong Kong Foodways

# Hong Kong Foodways

Sidney C. H. Cheung

Hong Kong University Press
The University of Hong Kong
Pokfulam Road
Hong Kong
https://hkupress.hku.hk

© 2022 Hong Kong University Press

ISBN 978-988-8754-35-9 (*Paperback*)

British Library Cataloguing-in-Publication Data
A catalogue record for this book is available from the British Library.

Digitally printed

# Contents

# Illustrations

# Preface

The great variety of food found in Hong Kong is known to people around the world, and restaurants/eateries can be found at every corner of the city. In Hong Kong, people can enjoy food from different countries, including those that are more traditional and others that are newly invented with creative skills and exotic ingredients. In reality, there are more Cantonese Chinese restaurants in the city, but the increase of non-Cantonese and non-Chinese restaurants can indeed reflect not only the changing eating habits of Hong Kong people but also the dynamics of socio-political development of our society in the last century. Therefore, when we talk about Hong Kong foodways, we are referring not only to the physical aspects of food in terms of form, taste, and texture, but also to mode of production, meanings of locality, traditional values, ideas, social change, and cultural identity.

Regarding the different kinds of Chinese regional cuisines that we can find in Hong Kong, people are always interested in their authenticity. Are they authentic traditional dishes, hybrids, or modified food for the local interest? It is not possible to give an answer in a few sentences, but I think the Cantonese cuisine we have in Hong Kong is relatively authentic with some changes based on the social and cultural developments. For example, the extensive use of lard or animal fat is not commonly seen in Hong Kong because people have become more health conscious. However, the non-Cantonese cuisines found in Hong Kong are closely related to migrant groups, who are particularly concerned about how and why the culinary skills have been inherited and used. Therefore, it is not surprising to see that some hybrid Chinese food with local styles were developed in Hong Kong when there were various influxes of specific groups to the society. For example, Shanghainese dishes served to the Cantonese public could be very different from those consumed by the Shanghainese migrants and their families. And the development of non-Chinese food is intriguing; it would be interesting to find out when, why, and how non-Chinese cuisines were adopted and became popular in the city.

Hong Kong has been a growing migrant society since the early twentieth century. What has affected Hong Kong's foodways? Was it the 1997 handover? Will the city's relations with mainland China and other countries play a role in the future? Again, issues such as heritage, conservation, lifestyles, well-being, and urban development will have impact on the foodways in Hong Kong as well. In order to provide a comprehensive picture of the development of Hong Kong foodways during the last century, this book will describe changes, variations, and innovations of Hong Kong foodways, and will pay particular attention to questions related to the context of changing lifeways and social tastes since the post-war era. I would like to broaden relevant classic work by examining Hong Kong foodways in different periods of the social development. In doing so, I look to advance anthropological inquiries by addressing recent theoretical issues concerning identity, migrations, consumerism, globalization, and the invention of local cuisines in the context of Hong Kong as a fast-changing society in East Asia.

I have revised most of my research findings for this book. Some of the findings were published previously in different academic journals and edited volumes. I hope this can be a milestone of my food research in Hong Kong. For someone like me who once aspired to be a filmmaker, I treat each published article as a short film and hope that it will show my readers the social reality and provide them a new perspective. I am particularly interested in working on a trilogy that I can build from my previous work with new developments. This is the model I have used for my earlier works, which include the studies of Ainu people's images (Cheung 1996, 2000a, 2004), Ping Shan Heritage Trail (Cheung 1999, 2000b, 2003), wetlandscape (Cheung 2007, 2008, 2011), and crayfish consumption (Cheung 2015a, 2015b, 2017). This book, however, is far more than a trilogy because it ranges across my earlier reseach on freshwater fish farming, Hakka restaurants, *nouvelle* Cantonese cuisine, *puhn choi*, and my recent studies of oyster cultivation and Hong Kong's Shanghainese food. I hope this book will provide fresh insights into the studies of foodways in Hong Kong as well as new topics to share while we enjoy Hong Kong food. Lastly, regarding the romanization of Chinese in the book, instead of using one system, I have used different systems including Wade-Giles, pinyin, and conventional Cantonese practices. I hope this will not cause too much trouble for the reader.

# Acknowledgements

I would like to thank all the people who shared with me their stories about food they produced, cooked, and ate. In addition, I would like to thank my family (Doris, Leni, and Ben), teachers (in Japan), friends, and fellow foodies, who helped make this book possible. In particular, a few friends inspired me in how to study food from an anthropological perspective: the late Sidney Mintz, David Wu, Tan Chee Beng, and James Watson. It has always been my pleasure and honour to know a lot of diligent farmers, ambitious food promoters, talented chefs, analytical food writers, and foodies with passions and curiosity, and they all have contributed to my study in many significant ways. Finally, I would like to acknowledge the generous help of the staff at Hong Kong University Press, the editorial work by Kristy S. Johnson, and the subvention provided by the Faculty of Arts at the Chinese University of Hong Kong for the copyediting of my manuscript.

# Introduction: Hong Kong Foodways

According to the *Merriam-Webster Dictionary*, the term 'foodways' is defined as 'the eating habits and culinary practices of a people, region, or historical period'. Eating habits are complicated because they are collective experiences instead of individual choices, while culinary practices can also be taken further to include relevant production, processing, distribution, consumption, and so on. Therefore, foodways significantly affect not only what we eat but also how, why, and under what circumstances we make our food choices both in the past and present. Since the 1970s, the term 'foodways' has been widely used by folklorists and anthropologists when food is addressed for the understanding of the cultural and socio-political meanings embedded in the practices of eating. Folklorist Jay Anderson argues in his PhD dissertation that foodways encompasses 'the whole interrelated system of food conceptualization and evaluation, procurement, preservation, preparation, consumption, and nutrition shared by all the members of a particular society' (Anderson 1971).

This background on the history and definition of foodways encompasses the scope of what I discuss in this book: the circumstances of production and consumption of food in Hong Kong society in the last century. I also highlight all the ecological, international, diasporic, and socio-political aspects of how our society has been developing with the involvement of its people in Hong Kong foodways. When one thinks of what makes Hong Kong different from other cities in the world, the colours of neon lights in the streets, crowds in the restaurants, and people's passion for eating and drinking with friends and families may come to mind. People's high expectations of fully enjoying food in Hong Kong may best be expressed in the old saying: 'A Heaven of Eating and Drinking'. However, the great variety of food in Hong Kong does not only involve decisions that must be made to choose the kind of Chinese, Asian, and Western food to be consumed; it also complicates relations with people's lifeways and values. How do we determine the meanings of food embedded in Hong Kong society, and how do they differ from those found in other Asian cities such as Tokyo, Taipei, Seoul, Singapore, and Beijing, where many different choices are also available? Apart from eating the basis for acquiring nutrients and satisfying the human instinct for survival, as in many societies, people in Hong Kong strongly regard food as one of the markers of their social status.

Today, in Hong Kong, there are many kinds of food ranging from cheap to expensive, ordinary to rare, and local to global. Apart from popular food such as Cantonese seafood, American fast food, Japanese sushi, and Korean barbecue, there are also various snacks sold as street food, luxurious high-class restaurant food, traditional festive food, and exotic foreign cuisine. Recounting the common types of food available in Hong Kong is not sufficient to even sketch the relations between food and culture in Hong Kong. Instead, it is necessary to understand what kinds of food are consumed by whom, and why? Although it is obvious that the logic behind food choice is different for different people, as one person's food can be another's poison, it is important to examine the meanings behind various kinds of food because they shape different people's choices. For example, we can see that some food items are well accepted by most people in many countries, while some food items are rejected in specific contexts (Martin 2001; Liu 2015). Regarding the reinvention of tradition in contemporary Hong Kong society, Cheng (1997) argues that the emergence of the modern herbal tea shop, with its strong emphasis on a sense of nostalgia, should be understood as part of the 'process of construction, maintenance, and negotiation of Hong Kong identity' (70–71). And, in a study of the meaning of Chiu Chow cuisine in Hong Kong, Lee (1997) suggests that popularity was achieved because of the success stories of the hardworking Chiu Chow people, who were well accepted by the Hong Kong public. They accepted an upgraded Chiu Chow cuisine serving as a metaphor for upward social mobility. Again, if *yumcha* can show how urban communication works in a Chinese restaurant with the enhancement of families and social networks (Lum 2013), then a tea café is definitely another kind of unique eatery model developed from the social and cultural needs of those from the grassroots (Chan 2019). Through the varieties of pineapple buns found in Hong Kong, Wang (2021) further demonstrates the ethnic and cultural complexities developed along the awareness of local identities from British colonization to the present.

Back to the history of the discipline, anthropological research in earlier studies on food and cuisine centred largely on questions of taboo, totems, sacrifice, and communion, shedding light on the approach of cultural symbolism, with an emphasis on how food reflects our understanding of humans and their relations with the world (Mintz 1996; Mintz and Du Bois 2002; Watson and Caldwell 2005). Previous structural anthropological research on edibility rules emphasizes not only why food is a symbol through which the *deep structure* of humanity can be investigated but also how corresponding concepts of commensality, edibility, body, and spatial territories can be discerned (Lévi-Strauss 1969; Douglas 1966; Tambiah 1969). More recently, scholars have broadened the studies on food, demonstrating it as an indicator of social relations, as gifts given at marriage banquets and other special feasts (Watson 1987; Kerner, Chou, and Warmind 2015), as a symbol of caste, class, and social hierarchy (Sahlins 1976; Goody 1982; Mintz 1985; Harris 1986), and as a metaphor through which the mechanism of self-construction can be discerned, particularly with regard to ethnicity and identity (Tobin 1992; Ohnuki-Tierney 1993; Wilk 2006b). Most importantly, among various ethnographies regarding ethnicity and identity in Asian countries, food is understood as a dynamic part of the way people think of themselves and others. During the last several decades, many studies on Asian material culture have used food to understand changes in the local dynamics of production, consumption, and social identity (Wilk 2006a; Cheung and Tan 2007; Klein 2007; King 2019).

In this light, many scholars interpret the localization of foreign food from a socio-political perspective (Watson 1997; Cwiertka and Walraven 2000; Wu and Tan 2001; Wu and Cheung 2002). These studies, in fact, confirm what Goody (1982) notes, that the emergence of *haute*/high cuisine developed within a context of growing industrialization, imperialism, and transnationalism through the changing social tastes occurring at the everyday level. Appadurai's (1988) research also demonstrates how foodways have been altered and how national cuisine, in fact, was invented within the colonial context. While there is no doubt that we can recognize a general kind of high cuisine formation in societies undergoing significant economic growth or socio-political transformation, we also observe that there are recently some local foods, prepared with traditional culinary skills and carrying regional characteristics, gaining popularity within a variety of venues. Whale meat consumption in Japan, the eating of dog meat in South Korea, the crayfish craze in mainland China, the Slow Food movement in Italy, and migrant families' homestyle cooking in Australia are examples of eating practices that play a role in resisting global forces by (re)constructing a sense of local-to-national identity at the everyday level (Duruz 2001; Leitch 2003; Cheung 2015b; Akamine 2021).

Another popular focus on food study concerns the meaning of being local, and there are several definitions of local in the context of production and consumption (Cheung 2019; Ho 2020). Firstly, food is most often defined as local when seen as evolving from traditional practices, ethnically or historically, or as a kind of family inheritance and emotional attachment. Secondly, being local also serves as a signifier of environmentally friendly choices such as having a low carbon footprint and being organic, seasonal, chemical free, natural, non-GM, and so on. Finally, local connotes a kind of slow production characterized as non-commercial, personalized, and involving regional characteristics. Such slow production stands in opposition to the mass production industry and market-oriented capitalism. Regarding the kinds of local food products in various cities around the world, most people may be surprised to see a very wide scope of varieties ranging from vegetables, fruits, honey, cheese, wine, seafood, preserved meat, and instant noodles. Similar situations can be found in Hong Kong society nowadays, and people pay attention to local food for many different reasons such as identity, nostalgia, or lifestyle (Ho 2020). With this in mind, then, it is important to illustrate how local food is culturally constructed in the fast-changing Hong Kong society.

When we look at how foodways are distinctive and unique for Hong Kong's Chinese majority, we can see the ways in which dietary change reflects the cultural construction of people's social lives. In classical studies of norms and traditions regarding how Chinese people choose food in various environments and circumstances, the most popular idea concerns the hot/cold dualism which is the maintenance of balance in the body by regulating the intake of certain foods. This relates to seasonal concerns in food choices such as hot food for keeping the body warm in autumn and winter, and cold food for keeping it cool in spring and summer. At the same time, people try to rid the 'humid and heat' (濕熱) of the body through the intake of herbal tea (涼茶) with various ingredients originally found in the local region. Also, there are traditional practices related to the consumption of seasonal food as it is harvested in nature; for example, people tend to eat fruits such as *laichee* and *long an* (also called dragon eyes) in July/August, crab in September/October, snake in early autumn, and other wild animals in winter. In addition, the balance of hot/cold and wet/dry food in people's diet tells us how eating habits are related to their conceptualization of the body in different conditions such as food restrictions in pregnancy and recovery from illness.

If the phrase 'we are what we eat' is true, then the next item on the agenda is one to examine in relation to how and what Hong Kong people actually eat. In this book, I pay more attention to the changes in foodways during the post-war era and examine how traditional kinds of food production and consumption have remained the same while also changed over time, and how new kinds of food have been introduced and localized in Hong Kong society. Apart from my research that focuses on food production and consumption, the theoretical framework of this book builds on the earlier works related to Hong Kong people's social life and thus to their constructions of self-identity during the pre-handover era. Furthermore, along with my recent ethnographic studies of Hong Kong's changing foodways in post-handover Hong Kong society, I have extended these inquiries to analyse how people shift their patterns of consumption and identity politics with such dramatic social and political transformation.

In Chapter 1, I set the structure for the book by introducing the local foodways based on Hong Kong's unique geographic location. Hong Kong is surrounded by rich fishing grounds on the east coast and protective aquaculture areas supporting carps, mullets, shrimps, and oysters, among others, on the north-west side, which is also the

Pearl River Estuary. In this chapter, I explain the long history of oyster cultivation and the emergence of the freshwater fish-farming industry in the original rice paddy area established since the mid-1900s.

Chapter 2 focuses on food brought in by migrants in the post-war era. The political economy of relevant food providers and consumers with the influx of post-war era migrants is elaborated in this chapter as well. I explain how Hakka restaurants were supported, due to a growing need for factory and construction workers at that time, and Shanghainese foodways were introduced both for the new community's own needs in food consumption and for the business development in the society.

The rise of Cantonese *nouvelle* and international cuisines—reflecting the modern and hybrid aspects of Hong Kong culture—is explored in Chapter 3. Since the late 1970s, Hong Kong society has successfully developed itself as the hub of international trading and finance and exhibited an obvious increase in living standards and much wider choices of foreign and luxurious products both for expats and local people. I examine the emergence of Cantonese *nouvelle* cuisine and incoming Japanese cuisine (as an example of international cuisine being accepted by the locals) to highlight the vibrant side of the society and the changing taste among the younger generations.

In Chapter 4, I discuss nostalgic food traced back to the 1990s, when Hong Kong people paid more attention to the history and tradition of the city. I use traditional village food and homestyle eating venues to explain how Hong Kong people reacted to cultural, economic, and political change and refashioned identities in the post-handover society. The two kinds of foodways—*puhn choi* (盆菜) and private kitchen food—illustrate the channels through which such marginal, rural, daily, and common foodways have played upon people's nostalgia for tradition, remembrance of the past, and an imagination of the *good old days* since the late 1990s.

Chapter 5 shows how the awareness of food has become a kind of cultural heritage since the last decade. With several food items and food systems listed as Hong Kong's Intangible Cultural Heritage (ICH) in 2014, the decision on regarding food as cultural heritage has been a popular topic among the general public. In this chapter, I investigate how Hong Kong foodways relate to heritage safeguarding and promotion by focusing on culinary resources in agricultural and cultivation systems, wholesale/retail trade networks, and the archival values of family recipes. My reason for highlighting the systematic aspects in the three cases featured is to show that food heritage is not only about the culinary skills; it also entails the transcended values embedded in the local social context for the benefits of global humanity. Again, based on my research in Hong Kong, I present the three case studies to draw attention to the paradox of defining heritage for preservation and the dilemma of whether traditional foodways should be preserved. In particular, I address those foodways which have been modified for market interest as they are often discredited for a loss of authenticity, although this is due, most likely, to the common challenges that many societies have been facing.

The last chapter concludes with a summary of concepts about the sociocultural meanings of commensality, food consumption, and well-being in Hong Kong to show how and what people in this fast-changing society have experienced through the practices of eating with the increasing demands for health, safety, and political integrity.

# 1
# Local Food Production

To understand the local food production supporting the traditional part of Hong Kong foodways, it is necessary to pay attention to the ecological characters and geographical location of Hong Kong. In French, the word *terroir* was commonly used to connote a complete natural environment in which a particular wine is produced with specific soil, topography, and climate. Even though the context might be different between France and Hong Kong, it is a kind of landscape we might want to have in mind while talking about the local food, specifically related to the production and consumption at some points.

In the late Qing period, Hong Kong was part of *Hsin-an* County in Guangdong Province but was taken as a British colonial possession in the middle of the nineteenth century. Hong Kong Island was ceded to Britain in 1842 in the Treaty of Nanking after the First Opium War (1839–1842). Kowloon was ceded to Britain in 1860 after the Second Opium War (1856–1860), and the New Territories were leased to the British government by the Imperial Chinese government for ninety-nine years in 1898. There were four major groups of inhabitants of traditional settlements in the New Territories who had ancestors settled there before the British took over in 1898, and are considered indigenous inhabitants to the New Territories, namely Punti (本地), Hakka/Punti

Hakka (客家/本地客家), Tanka (蜑家), and Hokklo (鶴佬). Punti and Hakka had their village settlements in different parts of the New Territories, while Tanka and Hokklo were identified as boat people (水上人), even though most of them are living on land nowadays.

Geographically speaking, Hong Kong is located at the lower basin of the Pearl River estuary on the west and is connected to the deep sea on the eastern coastline, being a place with rich resources from both nature and a long history of cultivation traditions. Some centuries ago, with the efforts of both Tanka and Hokklo who practised fishing for many generations in the area, Hong Kong society enjoyed a good supply of fishes caught in the nearby onshore area; even today, there is a high percentage of imported fish from both mainland China and Southeast Asia. Being a convenient spot for goods imported from the north and south (commonly called Nam Bak Hong, 南北行 in Chinese), Hong Kong has been an international trade hub for dried products as well. Apart from the ecological and geographical characters, Hong Kong is also a renowned migrant city in which there are a wide range of food varieties brought through migrants either as their own everyday life necessities or for generating incomes. These relevant phenomena are not only limited to the large influx of refugees after the 1949 liberation brought by Communist retribution on the Mainland but also the coming of Hakka settlers in the early Qing dynasty. Before looking into the issue of how food was inherited and brought to the society, I would like to start with looking at the kind of food available because of Hong Kong's special geographical location—the practices of oyster eating.

Oyster eating has interesting cultural significance in Hong Kong and South China; dried oyster (蠔豉) has been served not only as a seasonal (winter) delicacy but also as a fortune food for the Lunar New Year and plays the unusual role of vegetarian food in seasonal traditional events such as the First Day of Lunar New Year (農曆大年初一) and local Taoist (Daoist) events such as Cheung Chau Jiao

Festival, commonly called Cheung Chau Tai Ping Qing Jiao (長洲太平清醮) while animal killing is forbidden during the ritual of purification. Like the odd categorization of oyster as vegetable, there are legendary explanations of oysters growing from *seeds*, and of it being eaten by Buddha while suffering from starvation, and so it is accepted as food for fasting. As for the daily usage and consumption, oyster sauce (蠔油) is a well-known flavouring widely used in Cantonese cooking and has been developed as a famous brand name both nationwide as well as worldwide. Another important local product is the golden oyster (金蠔), a kind of half-dried oyster fried with sugar or syrup. It is considered a local seasonal gourmet food only available during December and January. I want to emphasize the fact that oyster cultivation has a long history in the Pearl River estuary and is one of the main traditional means of aquaculture that depends strongly on the natural coastal resource. Therefore, apart from the agricultural knowledge inherited through the coastal communities over the centuries, oyster cultivation is also embedded in the long-term, socio-economic relationships among various stakeholders in our society.

Nowadays, many daily food ingredients that we consume are in fact global in origin, but oyster cultivation has a strong local root because of the expected variation of salinity, temperature, and diversity of infauna organisms for the aquaculture practice. Oyster cultivation has a long history in different parts of the world, and relevant communities have rich experience with the quality and quantity controls for the long-term as well as sustainable coastal resource management, together with the strong emphasis on responsibility in safeguarding and promotion of the agricultural traditions among relevant coastal communities.

A brief overview of the aquacultural context would help us understand oyster as a crop. Oyster is a bivalve mollusc with hard shells, increasing in size as it grows. It belongs to the *Ostereidae* family with three genera: *Ostrea*, *Crassostrea*, and *Pyncnodonta*. *Ostrea edulis*, commonly known as European flat oyster, and *Crassostrea gigas*, commonly known as Pacific oyster, are the key species cultivated in Japan and northern coastal areas in mainland China. In Hong Kong, the two species cultivated in the Lau Fau Shan (流浮山, which literally means floating mountain) are *Crassostrea hongkongensis*, commonly known as white oyster (白蠔), which is also a unique species found in the area for which it was named, and *Crassostrea ariakensis*, commonly known as red oyster (赤蠔), differentiated by the colour.

There are some basic conditions for the growth of the oysters that are useful to know, which include, for example, temperature, salinity (5–30 ppt), and water quality required for different species, as well as cultivation methods, growing cycles, feeding systems, and purification after being harvested. Yet, for the same kind of oyster, the quality can be affected very much by the growing environments, including the setups and the processing. Regarding the oyster industry in Hong Kong, Morton and Wong (1975) explain the ecological characters of local oyster cultivation in the north-western side of Hong Kong as well as the Pearl River estuary as:

> The warm wet southeasterly monsoon in summer brings heavy rainfall to southern China increasing the discharge of the Pearl River, the Shum Chun River, the Yuen Long Creek and other small streams entering the bay. . . . The cool saline water in winter and the warm almost freshwater conditions in summer are particularly suitable for the cultivation of the Pacific oyster. (Morton and Wong 1975, 141)

Regarding the history of oyster eating in the Pearl River Delta area, archaeologists have found evidence of oyster consumption in South China for more than 3,000 years, based on the relevant layers of oyster shell. Again, there are also written documents from the Northern Song dynasty confirming the activities of oyster cultivation in the Pearl River area about 1,000 years ago. Apart from being one of the major animal proteins consumed by people at that time, oysters played important roles in various aspects of human lifestyles. For example, the shell has been used in Chinese medicine and was used extensively as building materials in the Qing dynasty. Regarding the massive oyster cultivation in the area, there is a legend about how local people discovered the skills, because oysters can only grow on the hard surface of rocks and broken potteries in the area.[1] I was told that local people used to drop rocks on the mudflat during the seedling period in order to facilitate the metamorphosis of oyster larvae (commonly called spat), and this practice is still going on despite the fact that they also buy oyster seeds for cultivation.

The Pearl River's oyster cultivation has taken place since the time of the Northern Song dynasty in the area where Guangzhou is located today (see Guo and Cheng 2006). However, it was because of the overdevelopment in the delta shore area causing large amounts of freshwater to collect during the rainy season to run directly into the basin, and as a result the upper basin became less and less salty over the years. In other words, the interface between marine water and river water was gradually pushed down to the south as well as the lower basin, which brought the oyster cultivation away from Guangzhou to the present Lau Fau Shan (流浮山) in the late Qing period.

Oyster farming in Lau Fau Shan can be dated back to over 200 years, and it has been an important cross-border industry between Hong Kong and Shenzhen, both of which are located at the lower basin of the Pearl River. In the past, oyster seeds were naturally collected and raised in the Lau Fau Shan, and mature oysters would be transferred to Shajing (沙井) in Shenzhen to be fattened for a few months before harvesting, given that the rainwater collected during the rainy season flew into the lower basin of the Pearl River Delta, providing a low salinity for the last stage of cultivation for the Chinese New Year consumption. However,

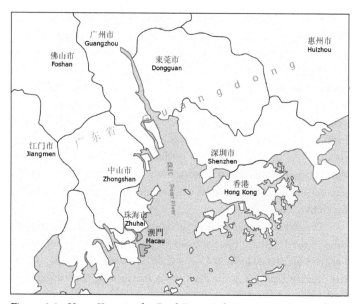

**Figure 1.1:** Hong Kong in the Pearl River Delta area. Map by Croquant: https://commons.wikimedia.org/wiki/File:Pearl_River_Delta_Area.

due to the political relations between Hong Kong and the Mainland, together with the strictly controlled border in the 1950s, oyster farmers in Hong Kong carried out all the operational stages on their own within Hong Kong territory, such as collecting spats, rearing, and fattening. Agricultural contamination (caused by the discharge of animal waste from pig farming) has been found in the Inner Deep Bay since the late 1960s. A lot of people thus felt reluctant to eat local oysters from the area. In the 1980s, to rid the area of such pollution, a floating barge (Japanese style) (Figure 1.2) was introduced instead of the traditional method as well as mudflat-level cultivation on the coastal areas. In 2018,

I was told by some major oyster farmers in Lau Fau Shan that they would install a new system with the financial support of government and technical advice from university researchers. With the new system, they hoped to regain consumer confidence in Hong Kong society by showing the safety of eating local oysters.

Hong Kong's north-eastern coast has a long history of commercial aquaculture because of its ecological advantages. However, it has been facing immeasurable threats due to many factors since the 1960s, such as agricultural and industrial pollution, infrastructure development, ageing of the local community, and market competition brought by the economic reform that has taken place in mainland China during the last few decades. At the same time, local people have been working against these difficulties, which include ageing, price competency from imported oysters, typhoons, and pollution; their experiences of maintaining the local traditions/industry should not be overlooked as similar challenges and disasters do happen in many other countries with similar setups. Although the significance of coastal community

**Figure 1.2:** Floating barge for oyster cultivation. Photo by Miriam Lee.

studies in Hong Kong on a broader scale is widely available, there is only limited research that helps us understand the coastal fishing/oyster industries in relation to community development, especially with regard to how local techniques and knowledge have been inherited as well as the socio-economic impacts experienced over the decades (Morton and Wong 1975).

Recently, the young generation of oyster farmers actively participated in various kinds of protection activities for oyster production. To rebuild the reputation of local Lau Fau Shan oysters, I witnessed how a local oyster culture-related NGO was set up to carry out the mission of promoting history and ecology of Lau Fau Shan. Regarding technical issues linked to food safety and marketing strategies, I observed that local oyster farmers were working with relevant governmental units to install new purification systems for bacteria control of fresh oysters cultivated in Lau Fau Shan. They also joined local farm festivals to promote their oysters to the general public, together with other agriculture and aquaculture products. According to what I observed, they joined the festival in 2017, and their products became popular among local residents who knew the reputation of Lau Fau Shan oysters even before they visited the place. It was the goal of local farmers to promote eating raw oysters from the area, but the concern of contamination has been a major obstacle for promoting local harvest in the form of dried oysters and fresh ones for cooking (such as deep-fried oyster) (see Figures 1.3 and 1.4). Since Hong Kong people have a strong awareness of the importance of oyster farming and eating as part of their cultural heritage, the dilemma between food safety and heritage will be around for a while. Given that oyster farming is closely related to the surrounding environment, it might be a challenge for us to rethink the vulnerability and resilience of the coastal community in Lau Fau Shan as a worldwide issue.

**Figure 1.3:** Dried oyster (with the golden oyster on the top and other dried oysters)

**Figure 1.4:** Deep-fried oyster

In addition to oysters as a seasonal food, Hong Kong's stable year-round food production in the area has been fish and rice. In fact, the phrase 'Homeland of Fish and Rice' (魚米之鄉) has been used to indicate the richness of the food production system in the Pearl River Delta area, as the daily diet of Hong Kong people consists of freshwater fish, which are consumed substantially, especially in families with elderly members. These dishes include, for example, steamed fish (grass carp) belly with ginger and scallions (薑葱蒸魚腩), steamed fish head (big head) with younger ginger and black soybean (子薑豉汁蒸魚頭), dried fish cake (煎魚餅), stuffed peppers/eggplant/tofu with minced fish (mud carp) (煎釀三寶), fish soup, and sliced fish for different kinds of congee. So, it is important to know how and when these freshwater fish were cultivated on the north-western side as well as the Inner Deep Bay of Hong Kong.

Historically speaking, in the Inner Deep Bay, there are traditional as well as local (本地) lineage settlements which can be traced back to 800 years ago, and the relevant agricultural (rice cultivation) practices are supposed to have lasted for several hundred years. In the early part of the last century, besides those inland agricultural areas, a major conversion of coastal wetland into agricultural land took place in Tin Shui Wai (天水圍), which went through different stages including mudflats, rice paddies, reed fields, shrimp ponds, and fishponds. Agriculture is not a major industry in contemporary Hong Kong society; however, it does not mean that its economic contributions should not be explored. As the history of fisheries reflects the social development and cultural change in Hong Kong, it is important to strive for a holistic understanding of the industry in the past and the present. The continuity of coastal development in the north-western part of Hong Kong has undergone various changes, and the emergence and commercial development of fishpond farming began in the 1920s and continued until the 1950s when there was a rapid growth of population and food demand. As large areas of farmland were converted into fishponds, the situation continued until the 1970s.

In Hong Kong, over 90 per cent of the freshwater fish farms are engaged in polyculture (e.g., grey mullet, bighead carp, silver carp, common carp, grass carp in combination with tilapia or snakehead). In a traditional fishpond, grass carp and grey mullet usually live in the upper zone as they like to forage and stay near the water surface. Bighead carp, silver carp, and tilapias like to float in the middle zone, while at the bottom, common carp and spotted snakeheads reproduce in the fishpond since both carnivorous fish are used to control the number of tilapias and other animals with less economic value. Polyculture systems have been used as a traditional model for freshwater fish farming inherited from other parts of the Pearl River estuary area, such as Shunde and Zhongshan. In Hong Kong, the history of commercial fish farming is about one hundred years old, starting from the 1920s. The scale and structure of fish farming in the marsh has been changing over time. There is no doubt that the relationship between farmers and the market was quite simple and direct before the 1950s.

Technically speaking, it is common to convert mudflats into paddy fields or fishponds for various kinds of agriculture and aquaculture, and the north-western part of Hong Kong is no exception. Agriculture has a long history in the area; settlements began to develop since the environmental conditions and the subtropical climate supported harvesting of two crops in a year. The traditional freshwater fishing industry, however, only dates back to the 1920s when most of the agricultural land was rice paddies, which included white rice cultivated by freshwater and red rice cultivated in the brackish area. Before the commercialization of freshwater fish farming, fishponds originated as *fung shui* (geomancy) ponds in many local villages; grown fish were caught and shared among lineage members. Lineage refers to people who identify themselves with the same ancestry and live in the same village with a common ancestral hall for the practice of worship and can be commonly found in most of the traditional settlements in South China. There were around a hundred hectares of fishpond land in 1940 (Lin 1940), while the brackish fishpond area was small before the 1940s. Starting from the mid-1940s, Inner Deep Bay became the main site for cultivating shrimp, grey mullet, snakehead, and other freshwater fishes, and it has continued to be a major source of freshwater fish for domestic consumption.

Due to the shortage of written documents and formal archival collection, my field research began with interviewing people about their knowledge of the origins of freshwater fish farming in the area. Instead of selling or exchanging the harvest, grown fish were caught and shared among lineage members. It was further learned that the commercialization of freshwater fishponds in Yuen Long and the northwestern New Territories began in the 1920s, especially in such areas as Shan Pui Tsuen, Wang Chau, Nam Shan Wai, and Tin Shui Wai. I will elaborate on this in the following paragraphs.

Shan Pui Tsuen (山貝村) is an indigenous, single-surname village located near the Yuen Long Old Market and is owned by the Lams. It is surrounded by fishpond land and, as Fung (1996, 62) describes, 'Fishpond farming began to gain popularity in Shan Pui Tsuen in the 1930s. Rainwater diluted the salinity of the pond water, making it possible to rear different species of fish. Still later, fish nurseries such as Tai Lee Co. emerged, making Yuen Long a fish-producing centre in Hong Kong.' Although some of these fishponds are no longer in use and have been reclaimed for residential purpose, the village of Shan Pui Tsuen played an important role in the development of freshwater fish cultivation and trade in the 1930s. From the data collected in my field studies, the Shan Pui Lams were significant not only because they had pond land for cultivation, but also because they played important roles in the promotion of fishpond cultivation in the post-war period.

These days, the Lams no longer practise fisheries; most of them are living either outside the village or overseas. To understand the history of freshwater farming in the area, I collected some information from the Chinese news archive. For example, according to a Chinese daily newspaper, *Huaqiao Ribao* (華僑日報), which reported the situation in Nam Pin Wai on 20 September 1958, Nam Pin Wai's fishponds were Kam Tin Tangs' ancestral property, and the earlier tenants were actually Shan Pui Lams.

Wang Chau (橫洲), another important location, was also reported to be one of the original sites of freshwater fish cultivation in Hong Kong. The owner of Tai Lee Company was Mr Ho, who was a non-indigenous Wang Chau resident. The construction of fishponds was assumed to start off the company's freshwater fish cultivation business. As Suen (1955, 4) reports, '[i]n 1930, Tai Lee Co. spent more than $120,000 in constructing thirteen ponds covering an area of three hundred mows. The greatest pond (about sixty-two mows) in Un Long [Yuen Long] belongs to this company.'[2] According to these earlier studies, half of the fishpond was located in Wang Chau and the other half was in Kam Tin (錦田), an area with one of the longest histories of long lineage settlements (Suen 1955). As for the fishponds in Nam Shan Wai (南生圍), Yeung (1968, 10) states, '[t]he fish farm was constructed around 1927. Before it was turned into a fish farm, the area was swampy and of little value to agriculture because the brackish soil there is not suitable for most crops or plants.'

According to Lin's 1940 article, there were five big fish-farming groups during the early development of this industry; 'each with an area of 100 to about 500 mows or 20 to 100 acres, were constructed in the low swamps on the south border of Deep Bay near Un Long Market. As in the case of saline and rice fields, they are enclosed by high dykes to prevent flooding at high tides or by storms or by heavy rain' (Lin 1940, 165). Lin (1940) also adds:

It is estimated that the total number of ponds owned by the six fish farms of Un Long districts cover an area of about 1,300 mows or 260 acres, of which 300 mows belong to the Tai Lee farm, 500 to the Poon Yau, 100 to the Leng Sang, and 200 to the Man Fong Cheng farm. If other small solitary ponds are included there would possibly be 1,500–1,800 mows altogether in the New Territories. At present only 30 mows of the 500 mows owned by the Poon Yau farm are actually used for fish rearing, the rest though completed have not yet been stocked. (169)

Based on Lin's mentioned information, there were 2,800–3,100 mows (about 500 acres or 200 hectares) of fishpond land in 1940.[3] Apart from a portion of lineage-owned fishponds cultivated for their members' consumption rather than for commercial trade, commercially farmed fishes were consumed locally. Lin (1940, 188) goes on to note:

The Un Long people, regard the grey mullet as a fish of the highest delicacy and a large portion of the local pond production is used to satisfy the local market demand. Unless the price in Hong Kong is much higher than that in Un Long, the locally produced mullet seldom come to the former market for sale. The other pond fishes also are mostly consumed by local people in the New Territories.

It must be stressed that fish fry exportation did not merely start after the Second World War, as Lin indicates (1940, 176):

There is one fry-dealer in Un Long who possesses about 10 ponds entirely devoted to fry raising. . . . In 1939, in a 5-mow pond he reared about 10,000,000 fry for one and a half months with success. Many of these fry were subsequently exported to Java, Malaya and Thailand.

Large-scale fishpond farming probably began after the Second World War, when increasing demand for fish was paralleled by the rapid increase in land for fishpond cultivating. Grant (1971, 36) reports that the fishpond area rose from 500 to 2,000 acres between 1958 and 1968. Furthermore, according to Fung: 'During 1954–55 period when the Chinese Government in the Mainland restricted export of any kind of fish fry to Hong Kong, attempts had been made to stock Tilapia instead of Chinese Carp in the New Territories ponds' (Fung 1963, 78). Therefore, the replacement of the shortage of imported fish by the expansion of local cultivation might be an explanation for the rapid increase in fishpond areas during that period.

Between the 1950s and 1970s, several important changes took place in the fishing industry. For example, the fish auction system was introduced in 1950; the Hong Kong New Territories Fish-Culture Association (HKNTFCA) was established in 1955; the Hong Kong population grew, creating an increasing demand for fish over these two decades; fish fry was exported until the late 1970s; and duck farming began in fishpond areas as well up until the early 1990s. As Lai and Lam (1999) report:

> From the 1960s to the early 1980s, the industry expanded rapidly in response to an upsurge in demand due to a population explosion in Colonial Hong Kong. In this golden age of the industry, local production contributed as much as 10–16 per cent of the total local consumption of freshwater food fish. Nevertheless, since 1985 a period of secular decline has set in. The resumption of agricultural land devoted to fishponds for suburbanization, the increase in costs of production and the availability of abundant cheaper substitutes from Mainland China are threatening the survival of the local pond fish industry. Both the area of land devoted to freshwater food fishponds and the total local fish output have been declining since the mid-1980s. (Lai and Lam 1999, 257)

On the other hand, the Agricultural, Fisheries and Conservation Department (AFCD) reported that they had imported new species to help local farmers compete with low-cost fish imported from the Mainland. However, there was insufficient demand for these species in the local market, and most of the local supply is limited to grey mullet, grass carp, tilapia, and big head. In the last few decades, in order to boost revenue from fish farming, freshwater fish farmers cultivated popular marine fish, upscale fish, and new imported species. The AFCD imported sea bass into Hong Kong in 1987–1988; milkfish in 2000–2001; Australian jade perch, tench, or doctor fish (Tinca tinca); Chinese long snout catfish in 2002–2003; and hybrid striped bass and sleepy cod in 2004–2005. However, there was limited innovation for the enhancement of local polyculture, and the only relevant technique of artificial bleeding was introduced in 1968–1975, mainly for grass carp and big head.

To highlight the changes that took place before freshwater fish farming was substantially practised in Hong Kong, I would like to demonstrate the relevant transformation through the example of Tin Shui Wai (天水圍). Currently, Tin Shui Wai is one of the highly populated new towns in Yuen Long. There were about 450 hectares of stream-screening ponds with paddy fields before they were converted into commercial fishponds and now this area is only recognized for its modern residential appearance. The history of Tin Shui Wai is interesting, although there is not much data about its development from mudflat to residential areas. According to Da Silva (1977, 50–52), the reclamation reflects some special socio-political backgrounds of the British colony:

> In 1911 the reigning dynastic government of Ching China collapsed, and China became a republic. In the wake of unrest following the founding of the republic a substantial number of

moneyed families sought refuge in relatively stable British Hong Kong. . . . The Hong Kong Government saw in the reclamation proposal submitted by the Chui brothers the opportunity to weaken further the power of the Tang lineages, especially that of Ha Tsuen village. . . . The Hong Kong authorities acceded to the reclamation proposal submitted by the Chiu brothers. An agreement was drafted in 1916 between Luen Tak Company and the Hong Kong Government whereby, for only a token rental, lease title for reclaiming four hundred and ninety and a half hectares of Ha Tsuen Wan was given to the company.

In other words, the land of Tin Shui Wai, located in Ping Shan, was owned by the Chiu family—founder of the Luen Tak Fish Farm (聯德魚場)—and not the Ping Shan Tangs, whose family settled there several centuries ago. According to my earlier interview with a retired officer working for the rental management of Luen Tak Fish Farm, Tin Shui Wai, which included white rice cultivation in the upper river (merely freshwater) and red rice (a kind of rice grown in fields with low salinity) cultivation near the coast. The farm was developed as rice fields in the 1910s. With the water gateway control (locally called *gei wai*, 基圍 in Chinese) for red rice cultivation, fish fry and shrimp fry were introduced and caught while sea water flowed to maintain the salinity for red rice cultivation. As red rice production declined, the red rice paddies were turned into shrimp farms; most of these farms were subsequently converted into fishponds in the 1970s. Another major change from rice paddy to vegetable farms was mentioned by Potter (1968), who showed the important connection between lineage systems and food production in the context of industrial development in Hong Kong.

It is important to understand the rice paddy mechanism that combines white rice and red rice in the upper and lower areas of Tin Shui Wai. Gated ponds in the brackish water, locally known as *gei wai*, were built to capture river water flowing down from the upper level; this way, sea water could be introduced to the red rice paddies. As shrimp farmers did not feed the shrimp, the operation cost was very low. In interviews with some retired shrimp farmers, I was told that they did not need to do much work but merely had to control the water quality through the operation of the water gateway. With this natural way of cultivation, the size of the *gei wai* is large and the density of shrimp kept inside is low. The operation is basically dependent on the availability of shrimp fry on the coast, which are taken into the *gei wai* during the high tide (with a low water level inside the *gei wai*), where the shrimp fry will be kept and fed for about nine months until they are big enough to be harvested. Farmers harvest the shrimp in the evening when they come up from the bottom, and water in the *gei wai* is drained during the low tide (or when the inside water level is higher than the outside); thus, shrimp will be caught in the net set at the gateway. Since the shrimp grow in the *gei wai*, Hong Kong people call them *gei wai* shrimp with the understanding that they grow in the brackish water. Other than the use of the *gei wai*, the farming operation is very natural. However, my informant told me that they used to reduce the density of the mangroves outside the gateway to make way for a smooth flow of shrimp fry into the *gei wai*.

Considering the close relations of local lineages and the changing land use in Tin Shui Wai, in the beginning of the last century, the British government anticipated resistance from local lineages and saw the necessity for a long-term stable administration in the New Territories. Therefore, soon after the British takeover, in order to weaken possible alliances among local villages, the government brought in outsiders and built a police station in the Ping Shan area (Cheung 2003). Nowadays, we no longer see the agriculture of rice, shrimp, and fish production in Tin Shui Wai. While the southern side is mainly for residential settlement, the northern side, where the Hong Kong Wetland Park is, has been very popular since its opening in 2006. The history of relevant food cultivation in the marsh should not be overlooked because the farming and cultivation at that time was an important prototype of our local food. With the dominant cases of oyster, rice, and freshwater fish cultivation in the north-western side of Hong Kong, local food production has been fully intertwined with the socio-political changes in Hong Kong and the complicated relations with south China regarding the trading relations, logistics, infrastructure, and probably the recent discussion on the overall future development in the Greater Bay Area.

This brings us to a brief overview of the current context. Since the beginning of the twenty-first century, organic farming and aquaponics have become more popular, and, currently, more people are willing to buy these products even though they are more expensive than the others farmed with conventional methods. During the last decade, a new era of local food production started and more people committed to local agriculture because of its contributions to food safety in our society. Therefore, we might have to admit that the existing products supplied as local food production have already lost their role in terms of food security for meeting the demands of the population's needs. However, the new role of enhancing people's knowledge about food safety has become more significant than any time in the past.

In Chapter 2, I discuss the migration issues that brought new eating habits to Hong Kong, especially during the post-war period, as well as the dynamism of foodways in the fast-changing city.

# 2

# The Arrival of Migrants' Food in the Post-war Era

Hong Kong is a migrant society, even though the majority of its population speak Cantonese, a southern dialect spoken in several provinces in South China. During the last eighty years, Hong Kong underwent drastic population changes in urban development due to both economic growth and changing political relations with mainland China. As a result of two large-scale, post-war immigration waves from 1945 to 1947 and 1949 to 1952, Hong Kong's population grew from 600,000 in 1945 to 2,340,000 in 1954. The migrants included Hong Kong residents who had previously fled the three years and eight months of Japanese occupation and those from mainland China who left after the Communist Revolution in 1949. Apart from increasing the labour force, the latter group brought capital, skills, and an urban outlook, which provided human capital that met the needs of Hong Kong's economic system at that time. However, the overloading of migrant populations in the squatter settlements caused vulnerable conditions, which led to the 1953 Shek Kip Mei fire and accelerated the long-term public housing development in Hong Kong. Eventually, with the stability offered by the new housing policy for most working-class people, a large low-cost labour force emerged and helped to develop Hong Kong's light industry.[1] Among the many kinds of career skills brought by the incoming migrants, restaurant work was probably one of the most common options, as it provided stable income while the migrant workers gradually adapted to the new environment.

It is impossible to address all the Cantonese and non-Cantonese migrants who had come to Hong Kong in the last seven decades. However, it is meaningful to see the diversities of foodways they brought for their own interests/consumption and for commercial purposes in relation to how the varieties became the foodscape in the local culture. My research focused mostly on two groups—Hakka and Shanghainese. Both were distinctive in the ways they shaped local eating habits. Before exploring the contribution of these two groups in depth, I would like to focus on the Shandong chefs who indeed brought something special to the Hong Kong society.

It is widely known that Chinese foodways consist of a complex mix of regional ingredients and culinary skills, comprising a system of knowledge not only inherited from the past but also determined by socio-political changes in different eras. Even though great differences can be found between northern and southern ingredients and culinary skills, there are also common characteristics shared among the cuisines in various regions through internal migration and the importation of ingredients and cooking skills. Thus, different regional cuisines have their own development in terms of changing tastes and styles of presentations. Chinese food has been commonly classified into four major regional cuisines: East, West, North, and South. The northern cuisine, famous for its cooking skills, is represented by the early establishment of the Shandong cuisine which influenced the Imperial Court cuisine as well as the later Beijing cuisine. However, the Shandong community in Hong Kong used to be very small, and the Shandong cuisine has not been popular among Hong Kong Cantonese residents. Apart from the local interest, though, the Beijing cuisine attracted overseas visitors who might have been unable to travel to mainland China after the 1950s.

Therefore, it is not surprising to find many well-known Peking (Beijing) restaurants such as Spring Deer (鹿鳴春), American (美利堅), Lok Kuen Lau (樂宮樓), Chung Chuk Lau (松竹樓), Tai Fung Lau (泰豐廔),[2] and Peking Restaurant (北京酒家), in which Shandong chefs were hired for cooking Beijing cuisine such as Peking duck and fresh handmade noodles, particularly in front of tourist customers. Interestingly, apart from the typical Beijing dishes such as Peking duck and deep-fried fish, some food items such as Shandong roasted chicken (山東燒雞), Shandong big bun (山東大包), and deep-fried banana (拔絲香蕉) remained as good memories of the visits for local people.

According to an interview I had with the owner of Chung Chuk Lau Peking restaurant in Causeway Bay, Shandong chefs came to Hong Kong and cooked Western food for bankers who had come to Hong Kong in the early 1950s, and most of these chefs started their own careers cooking Beijing food in the 1960s. This explains why the Shandong chefs working in those Peking restaurants played an important role in serving food to American and European tourists visiting the city in those days. Most of these restaurants are closed now, and Shandong chefs specialized in Peking cuisine are very hard to find. Nowadays, there are more locally trained Peking food chefs working in non-Cantonese restaurants. In contrast to the changes that have taken place in Peking restaurants, Hakka restaurants show another perspective of Hong Kong's social change and economic development with incoming migrants during the post-war era.

In their study of Chinese food and cuisine, both Anderson (1988) and Simoons (1991) point out that Hakka food, compared to other regional food, is simple, straightforward, well prepared, and without exotic or expensive ingredients. Hakka food, developed along the East River in Guangdong Province, became popular in Hong Kong soon after the Second World War. It developed as a representative cuisine during the 1950s and 1970s and survived with difficulty in the last several decades. Regarding their origin in Hong Kong, Hakka restaurants started in Shek Kip Mei (石峽尾) during the late 1940s and early 1950s when many Hakka people moved to Hong Kong and resided in the Shek Kip Mei squatter settlement. During that period, the Shek Kip Mei squatter settlement consisted of four villages: Shek Kip Mei village (石峽尾村), Pak Tin village (白田村), Wor Tsai village (窩仔村), and Tai Po Road village (大埔路村), all of which started out as farming communities. With the influx of refugees from mainland China after 1949, there were about 60,000 people living and working in this area by the early 1950s. There were domestic huts and cottage factories that produced rubber footwear, toys, torches, soaps, and other goods. Hakka restaurants in the area were opened by Hakka people who had migrated from Xingning (興寧) in Guangdong Province. So, why did they all come from the same area? Could they cook better than the other Hakka people? I think the answer is not about their culinary skills but the way they could get jobs at that time. In those days, if people wanted to get a job, they needed referrals. For people without formal qualifications, someone from the same hometown provided major credibility. Therefore, it was quite often that some jobs possessed a regional character in those days. And Hakka restaurants turned out to be one of those kinds.

In the mid-1990s, I interviewed several Hakka chefs who worked in different Hakka restaurants in the 1960s and 1970s. They told me that the kinds of Hakka food they made were mostly snacks, including fried large intestine, bean curd, and beef balls, although all these dishes were quite different from the Hakka cuisine we now have. The Hakka restaurants started by the Hakka people in the late 1940s were in business until the Shek Kip Mei Great Fire. In the following decades, Hakka restaurants spread to different areas; this development started a new chapter in the history of Hong Kong people's food culture. It is important to consider the corresponding changes in lifestyle in Hong

Kong after the great fire. Historically speaking, the Shek Kip Mei fire catalysed the development of public housing projects in Hong Kong. On the Christmas Eve in 1953, a total of 53,000 people lost their homes in the Shek Kip Mei fire. The subsequent rehousing work led to the development of Hong Kong's permanent multi-storey public housing system. Twelve months after the great fire, the Shek Kip Mei public housing estate was built. It was Hong Kong's first public housing estate, with a total of eight seven-storey, H-shaped housing blocks. Rehousing and the long-term housing policy that followed had a direct influence on family structures, living environments, job opportunities, and lifestyles. It was mainly because of the great fire that Hakka restaurants spread to different parts of Hong Kong.

From a culinary point of view, I think there are two reasons that Hakka food gained popularity in Hong Kong. First, it is eaten with rice, which is the staple food in South China; Hakka food was therefore easily accepted because of its similarity to Cantonese cuisine. Second, Hakka food is quite different from domestic food in Cantonese families in terms of taste, ingredients, and culinary skills. In its transformation from ordinary food to high cuisine (Goody 1982), key features of Hakka cuisine at the time included the exotic flavourings for the *umami* (e.g., sandy ginger powder 沙薑, preserved vegetables 梅菜, red wine residue 紅麴酒糟, and salty fish 鹹魚) with expensive ingredients (e.g., chicken, pork, ox bone marrow, and beef balls). The use of a large amount of meat was a good source of valuable animal protein that helped generate energy for the workers in the light industries, which flourished in the late 1950s. Thus, I believe that Hakka cuisine became popular because of its rich, salty taste and also due to meat, which was important for energy-demanding jobs that increased from the late 1950s to the 1970s. This also explains why chicken, pork, and beef balls became popular dishes in Hakka cuisine in the 1950s. Nevertheless, Hakka cuisine, as experienced in Hong Kong, should not be considered solely in terms of authenticity or originality. Rather, it should also be understood as a cuisine chosen and selected within a particular social context. At that time, a typical family diet consisted primarily of fish and vegetables. Hakka restaurants were places to satisfy a need for meat as well as animal protein with natural flavours—*umami* from fermentation. Other examples include: salty baked chicken (鹽焗雞; in the old days, chicken dishes were festive or for special occasions); pork stewed with preserved vegetables (梅菜扣肉; pork was considered a luxury item as well); and bean curd and minced pork with salty fish flavouring (釀豆腐; commonly recognized as a traditional Hakka dish). These dishes along with fried beef marrow with vegetables (骨髓扒三鮮), fried pig stomach with fermented rice residue (酒糟炒豬肚), beef balls (牛肉丸), and fried large intestine (炸大腸) are still popular dishes in Hong Kong. Not many people, however, know that these originated in Hakka cuisine and are closely related to the history of Hong Kong's social development.

If a relatively large group of Hakka migrants eventually became chefs for the working class in those days, Shanghainese migrants are a different story in the scope of Hong Kong foodways. There are studies on Shanghai entrepreneurs in Hong Kong's business history, but not much has been written about Shanghai migrants' social life and community development in Hong Kong. In Guldin's 1977 study on the Fujianese community in Hong Kong, a Shanghainese community was shown to have already formed in North Point before the Fujianese migrants came to Hong Kong in the 1950s. As Guldin (1977) mentions:

> [A] new wave of "Shanghainese" descended upon Hong Kong although even at this early date North Point was not the destination of all Shanghainese; the wealthiest went to the most exclusive areas of the colony while the bulk of the predominantly middle-class Shanghainese proceeded to North Point and lent a decidedly bourgeois flavor to the area. By 1950 "Little Shanghai"

> was well established. Restaurants, tailor shops, beauty parlors
> and other businesses were all set up by Shanghainese to serve
> the area's essentially Shanghainese population. . . . If there was
> ever a time that North Point had a majority non-Guangdongese
> population, this was it. (Guldin 1977, 113–114)

The fact that Shanghainese migrants lived close to one another is most likely related to linguistic and cultural issues, because most of them did not speak Cantonese and wanted to live in an environment where a convenient livelihood could be developed according to their needs. The infrastructure of North Point was largely enhanced after 1957, and geographically it was at a distance from major business and financial areas such as Sheung Wan and Central. Distance was probably why Shanghai migrants chose North Point as a destination. In addition to the language difference, Shanghai people differed from local Cantonese people in many ways. Firstly, even now, Hong Kong Cantonese people still consider Shanghai people to be 'northerners' who have a different culture, especially when compared to 'southerners', or most of the Hong Kong population. For example, when local people say 'Shanghai style' they usually imply that Shanghai people pay attention to their looks; they dress well, talk with exaggeration, and so on. Secondly, Hong Kong people tend to think that a lot of Shanghai people have worked as chefs, tailors, and barbers. Thirdly, regarding their foodways, Hong Kong people consider Shanghai cuisine closer to Beijing and Sichuan cuisines (again, they are considered 'the north'); even now, it is easy to find restaurants serving a mixture of Beijing, Sichuan, and Shanghai food in Hong Kong.

Shanghai migrants also made a significant contribution to the post-war economic development of Hong Kong. According to Johnson and Johnson's (2019) long-term study of Tsuen Wan, one of the earliest industrial towns in the New Territories: 'From 1948 onwards, such entrepreneurs, often from the Shanghai area, were a critical part of the migration from China to Hong Kong. . . . The Shanghai entrepreneurs brought not merely their capital and their own entrepreneurial talents, but very often their skilled workers as well' (2019, 75). Given that Shanghai had been developing as a modern city in the late Qing period, incoming Shanghai people brought not only resources and skills for Hong Kong's post-war light industrial development but also their established social networks and lifestyles. For example, two major institutions played important roles for the large inflow of Shanghainese migrants after the 1940s: resident associations, which helped migrants find jobs, and grocery shops, which supported their food preferences in Hong Kong.

The beginning of the second Sino-Japanese war in 1937 triggered large-scale migration from Jiangsu and Zhejiang to Hong Kong. This led to the establishment of various regional resident associations (同鄉會), fostering social networks and business partnerships. Common language and common places of origin created a zone of trust in a new environment. Understandably, this became meaningful for employment and for social life, including festivals and foods. At that time, one needed a referral as well as guarantee in the job market. Therefore, resident associations would help introduce more people from the same area to new jobs and provide support to one another in the unfamiliar Cantonese-speaking society. Also, people could find familiar food in resident associations, which was appreciated because most of them were not used to Cantonese food (Cheung 2020).

One notable early association of this kind was the Kiangsu Chekiang and Shanghai Residents (Hong Kong) Association (蘇浙滬同鄉會). It was established in 1946 and renamed in 2006 with the inclusion of Shanghai. The association is located on two floors of a commercial building in Central. Since 1969, the restaurant has operated on a membership system, and these days their members are well-off, but not necessarily Shanghainese. Given the fact that it has been one of the most upscale restaurants serving traditional Shanghainese cuisine, many non-members would enjoy their high-quality Shanghainese cuisine by using their friends' memberships. Another popular resident association famous for its restaurant is the Ning Po Residents Association (寧波同鄉會), which was established in 1967. Their restaurant has become a conventional restaurant that welcomes all walk-in customers. Another type would be the Shanghai Fraternity Association Hong Kong Limited (上海總會). Established in 1977, it has been a well-known restaurant for Shanghainese cuisine in town as well. These restaurants that were organized to celebrate and to preserve a region-based cookery driven by the sentiments of a native place (i.e., Shanghai) naturally made local Hong Kong people feel like outsiders.

Regarding the inheritance of Shanghainese food for culinary practices, it is beneficial to pay attention to the development of Shanghainese grocery stores, which used to be called Nan Fo Po (南貨舖), or southern product shops that support domestic and commercial productions of Shanghainese food in Hong Kong. They are different from most local groceries (雜貨舖) because they sell Jinhua ham, noodles, wine, kelp, condiments, and other products that cannot be easily found in local groceries. They play the role of a mini-market, selling seasonal items such as live hairy crabs, dumplings, mooncakes, and veggies, and it is still possible to find these groceries in old neighbourhoods such as Kowloon City, Sheung Wan, North Point, and Sham Shui Po. Most of them were established several decades ago, and the oldest one I know was founded in 1956 in Kowloon City. Therefore, because of the presence of resident associations and groceries, Shanghainese migrants could live in Hong Kong without losing the dietary practices with which they were familiar. Shanghainese migrants also earned their living by running restaurants for the local Cantonese. In the following section, I will illustrate how Shanghai cuisine came to Hong Kong and gave rise to new tastes for the local public.

The post-1949 migrants included Hong Kong residents who had previously fled the Japanese occupation and mainland Chinese who left China after the Communist Revolution in 1949. In addition to increasing the labour force, the latter group brought capital, skills, and an urban outlook, which provided human capital that met the needs of Hong Kong's economic system at that time. This led to enormous social development in the post-war era. In 1954, a long-term housing policy devised by the Hong Kong government raised the overall living standards of Hong Kong residents. With the stability offered by new public housing for most working-class people, a large low-wage labour force emerged and helped to develop Hong Kong's light industries. By the mid-1960s, Hong Kong had achieved great success in economic development; at the same time, the Cultural Revolution began in China and led to a period of great suffering and turmoil on the Mainland. The Hong Kong government started various local campaigns to create a sense of mutual belonging among people living in Hong Kong. Most scholars agree that it was in the late 1960s when a 'Hong Kong identity' emerged, especially after the riots of 1967 (Ma 1999). This identity developed more fully in the 1970s; campaigns such as 'Clean Hong Kong', 'Against Corruption', and the Hong Kong Festival are just a few examples. One further indication of a more defined Hong Kong identity was the popularity of using Cantonese in the mass media that began in the late 1960s, and the concomitant growth of a Cantonese-based popular culture. Before this time, English and Mandarin had been the dominant languages of the mass media in Hong Kong. The rise of Cantonese in the media had a profound impact as Cantonese movie production grew and even attracted worldwide attention in the 1970s.

Regarding the arrival of Hakka food, I think it should be considered a model in which certain appropriate items were selected for the host society's needs. The same model works for Shanghainese food, especially working-class food such as dumplings, steamed buns, and noodles. Most of these dishes were inexpensive and offered by restaurants with simple names such as 369, Big Shanghai (大上海), and Yat Pan Heung (一品香). Other more upscale restaurants had poetic names, such as Tin Heung Lau (天香樓) famous for Hangzhou cuisine; Snow Garden (雪園), Hu Jiang (滬江), and Lau Yuen (留園) for Shanghainese cuisine. I am not able to provide a comprehensive list of those restaurants because a lot of them have closed. From what can be observed in the restaurants that are still in business, they serve signature dishes in 'thick sauce with strong taste' (濃油赤醬) such as stewed pork knuckle, Dongpo pork, fried eel, drunken chicken, and tea smoked duck. I cannot even tell whether their dishes keep the original tastes or have been localized for local Cantonese customers. But most of them do not serve any Cantonese dishes in order to confirm the difference.

I would also like to point out that many of the upscale restaurants employed chefs who had inherited traditional culinary skills before coming to Hong Kong, and some famous restaurants established branches in Hong Kong, such as Lao Ching Hing (老正興). This restaurant was founded in Shanghai in 1862 and a Hong Kong branch was set up in 1955. However, the restaurant was closed in 1993 and was later rebranded the Old Shanghai (老上海) with a similar kitchen team. The restaurant still serves most of their signature dishes to this day. Inheritance of traditional culinary skills for new restaurants has been an important concern in Hong Kong's food industry, and Shanghainese restaurants are no exception. According to some media sources, chefs from renowned places or resident association restaurants have opened new restaurants in which traditional or signature dishes from earlier versions of the restaurants are served. These might help justify the authenticity of their food.

Apart from its signature dishes, which were known for their authenticity, Lao Ching Hing was also the first restaurant to import hairy crabs from Shanghai to Hong Kong. The Shanghai hairy crab, now a very localized food item for the Hong Kong people, is a kind of freshwater lake crab and different from the marine crab and mud (brackish water) crab commonly used in Cantonese cuisine. Steamed hairy crab is usually served as a seasonal delicacy in many upscale Cantonese restaurants. Another kind of highly localized Shanghainese dish would be the appetizers served at Cantonese banquets since the 1980s. Along with the formation of *nouvelle* Cantonese cuisine, the eight dishes of Jiangnan (江南八小碟)[3] were created as appetizers for high cuisine by a local celebrity chef. I was told that the introduction of these appetizers was due to the lack of appetizers in a regular Cantonese banquet, so Shanghai-style cold dishes were used to fill the gap. Nowadays, we can easily find these appetizers served in Cantonese restaurants, but few people know that they were indeed an invention of the 1980s.

Regarding the growth of Shanghainese food in Hong Kong, I put forth an interesting question about the differentiation between Huaiyang and Shanghainese cuisines in Hong Kong. How do people identify Huaiyang or Shanghainese cuisine, as they have been constructed differently and reflect the social changes in the cultural and historical context? Studies suggest that the demarcation between Huaiyang and Shanghainese cuisines is related to southern migration in the Southern Song dynasty (1127–1279). In other words, the population growth in the tenth and eleventh centuries enhanced not only the inflow of migrants to southern coastal regions but also the development of Zhejiang (Hangzhou was its capital in the Southern Song dynasty). Huaiyang cuisine was formed due to early economic and agricultural developments, and Yangzhou was one of the richest cities in China during the Tang dynasty (618–907). In the early Qing dynasty (1644–1911), the Customs House in Shanghai played an important role in Jiangsu's foreign trade. In 1854, the Shanghai Municipal Council was created, and its creation brought the city to its golden age in the

1920s (Wills 2011). With its modern development, Huaiyang cuisine became a crucial component in Shanghainese cuisine in the nineteenth century, which was a kind of high cuisine of the metropolis, through the selection of special dishes from the surrounding areas of Jiangsu and Zhejiang. These traditional dishes that had been enjoyed by Shanghainese metropolitans were brought to Hong Kong when the migration waves exploded in the late 1940s.

From my Hong Kong perspective, some dishes in Huaiyang cuisine do not seem to differ much from those in Shanghainese cuisine in terms of the ingredients used, seasoning, taste, and culinary style. Huaiyang cuisine is also considered sweeter (with the use of more sugar) and, compared to other Chinese regional cuisines, the dishes are cooked with thicker sauces and served with rice and noodles. Taking a closer look at the names of regional cuisines in the Jiangsu and Zhejiang areas, other cuisines can also be found in cities such as Hangzhou, Ningbo, Shaoxing, Nanjing, Suzhou, Wuxi, and Shanghai. However, the general name of Huaiyang cuisine has been selected to represent all dishes from these related culinary regions. In Hong Kong, Shanghainese represented the conflation of migrants from the Jiangsu and Zhejiang areas. Their differences from local Cantonese can be seen not only in the geographical location but also the lifestyles of the migrants and their descendants in Hong Kong. Therefore, instead of Huaiyang, which has been the categorization of cuisine, Shanghainese cuisine embraces a wider scope of lifestyles that are aligned with the identity constructed in the migrant society.

To summarize, the examples of Hakka and Shanghainese food discussed in this chapter are just the tip of the iceberg, given that there were so many migrants with different backgrounds and eating habits coming to Hong Kong in the post-war era. For example, the old neighbourhood in Kowloon City has been developed as a Thai community in which we can find Thai groceries, restaurants, and shops for religious objects, much like the Shanghainese model mentioned earlier. Vietnamese and Indonesian restaurants have followed the model of Hakka restaurants in gaining local interest. Yet, these are not the whole picture because there are also migrants serving street food such as Chiu Chow candy (糖葱餅), Hakka fried radish cake (炸油糍), and Shanghai fried pork bun (生煎包), and each is a piece of the tesserae used in the mosaic of Hong Kong's migrant history.

# 3

# The Rise of *Nouvelle* Cantonese and International Cuisines

In Hong Kong, food can be used as an important indicator of different ethnic groups. By comparing the staple foods, rice and congee, the ethnic differences between the Cantonese and the Fujianese can be examined. For example, Guldin (1979, 233–234) points out that:

> [o]lder Fujianese women will often subsist on little more than spinach, peanuts, and congee (rice gruel) and the other fare typical of the poorest in Fujian: sweet potatoes and salty melons. Older women will eat these foods on preference even in Hong Kong and even if the family can afford better. These older Fujianese firmly believe Fujianese food to be the best cuisine and rank Guangdongese only third in choice. . . . The traditional Fujianese custom of eating congee three times daily is yielding to the Guangdongese preference for rice, especially during lunch times on the job when congee is often unavailable.

This demonstrates both the varieties and ever-changing aspects of foodways in Hong Kong; Cantonese is the mainstream cuisine and there have also been various regional cuisines brought to the city by non-Cantonese migrants since the 1950s. Apart from the Shanghainese foodways mentioned in Chapter 2, Fujianese foodways can also be found in the same neighbourhood.

In the study of the North Point community that was taken over by the Fujianese after the Shangainese, Guldin (1979) points out that another difference between the Guangdongese/Cantonese and Fujianese is their frequency of having *yumcha*. *Yumcha* (飲茶) literally means 'drinking tea' and is a Cantonese-style breakfast taken outside the home with dim sum, or various kinds of snacks, as its principal feature. The origin of this eating style was from Guangzhou. Customers were mostly merchants and traders, and its main purpose was social rather than to simply satisfy hunger. *Yumcha* came to Hong Kong in the early twentieth century and was not widely popular at first. During the post-war era, especially in the 1950s and 1960s when Hong Kong experienced an influx of refugees from mainland China, *yumcha* was largely an activity of single men who met over their breakfast tea to socialize or exchange tips about job-seeking and bird rearing. At that time, men brought birds with them in small bamboo cages and chatted with other customers. This was the backdrop in Hong Kong tea houses (茶樓 or 茶室) and most were closed in the 1990s. Tea houses are different from the restaurants (酒樓 or 大酒樓) where we now go for *yumcha*. First, restaurants are usually bigger in size and located in crowded or busy areas. Some of them are even chain stores such as Maxim's, Treasure Seafood Restaurant, and Hon Po Restaurant. Some provide wedding and birthday banquet feasts for up to one hundred tables. Other restaurants also provide entertainment, and these are called restaurants with night clubs (酒樓夜總會). *Yumcha* has changed from being a venue for men to socialize to a gathering place for the entire family. Since *yumcha* restaurants are flexible enough to accommodate different numbers of participants, who can spend varying amounts of time, *yumcha* serves to draw together family members who may live and work in different parts of Hong Kong and hence reinforces the institution of the family. The changed function of *yumcha* reflects the full indigenization of a whole generation of early immigrants in Hong Kong society.

Another point to observe is the change in the *yumcha* menu. Much of the food eaten at *yumcha* was originally street food. It was made and eaten in the street rather than in restaurants. For example, fried rice rolls (煎腸粉), fried bread in rice rolls (炸兩), fried peppers/eggplant/tofu with fish meat (煎釀三寶), fish balls and pig skin (魚蛋豬皮), curried squid (咖哩魷魚), sweet sesame or red bean soup (豆沙糖水), and bean curd flower (豆腐花) all began as snacks sold in the street but have become popular dishes served in *yumcha* restaurants. This reflects an interesting underlying structural change in Hong Kong society; that is, there has been a large upward mobility of the lower working class and they have attained the so-called middle-class status within a few decades. Ironically, the food that people choose reveals the fact that even though people's taste moves from the street to the restaurant, the content of the food may not differ at all.

In contrast to *yumcha*, another unique Hong Kong–style eating establishment is the café, which is a typical example of Hong Kong's East-meets-West character. Tea cafés (茶餐廳) are small restaurants that sell both Western and Chinese food. They can be found in every Hong Kong neighbourhood and have a reputation for providing a wide range of food choices that are cheap and fast. Tea cafés are not only typical of Hong Kong as a melting pot for different cultures, they also produce characteristically Hong Kong foodstuffs which reinforce a unique Hong Kong identity that belongs to neither the Chinese nor the English cultures (Wu 2001). Drinks such as 'boiled coke with ginger juice' (薑汁煲可樂) and *yin yeung* (鴛鴦; the former is a special combination with a reputation for curing cold and influenza, and the latter is a mixture of coffee and tea with milk) both serve as good examples representing Hong Kong's complicated mixture of Western and Chinese characteristics. Toasted bread with omelette for breakfast, congee and noodles, barbecue pork/roasted duck on rice, and bakery goods among others form the unique combination of food being served in tea cafés. Most of the tea cafés are independent and small sized, but recently more tea café chain stores have appeared with their own market niche. From the drinks and food served in tea cafés, one can see a localization of Eastern and Western cuisines that rejects authentic food and drinks of both cultures in favour of a new, uniquely Hong Kong flavour. In other words, the localized Western food has always been a question when people start thinking about Hong Kong as a cosmopolitan city. For example, the most popular Hong Kong breakfast sets can be congee with fried noodles or scrambled eggs with sausage, but they can also be macaroni soup with ham (火腿通粉), or Japanese instant noodles with luncheon meat and fried egg (午餐肉煎蛋公仔麵 or 餐蛋麵). It might not be possible to know the origins of each hybrid food item found in the society; however, from a macro perspective, I see three significant trends for the incoming of Western foodways. Since the last decade, because of the increasing number of non-Cantonese as well as mainland customers, some tea café chain stores have been offering famous regional spicy items such as Sichuan boiled fish (水煮魚), chilli fried chicken (辣子雞), and fish with pickled vegetable (酸菜魚) in their lunch and regular menus. Apart from those regional spicy foods, Japanese eel with rice, Taiwanese minced pork with rice, and all-day English/continental breakfasts are available as well. Therefore, there is no doubt that all these changes in the menu show the flexibility and characters of tea cafés in Hong Kong.

The first trend of the incoming Western restaurants took place in the 1930s, and Tai Ping Koon (太平館) restaurant is representative of the influx. Tai Ping Koon was a family business founded in 1860 in Guangzhou. Because of the British and French culinary influences, they provided upscale Western dishes such as steak served with soy sauce–based gravy, deep fried pigeon, and smoked fish. Their Hong

Kong business only became substantial in the 1950s, and some of their signature dishes came to be icons of Hong Kong's Western foodways. These included Swiss chicken wings (legend has it that it is not an imported Swiss recipe but was made with a sweet sauce that was mispronounced as 'Swiss'), deep fried pigeon, pork chop, stewed ox tongue, ox tail soup, smoked sliced pomfret, comprador soup, chicken broccoli cream soup, and soufflé. Today, when one goes to a local Western restaurant for a set meal, one would likely be asked to choose between the 'white' soup or the 'red' soup before the main course is served. If the white soup is considered a relative of chicken broccoli cream soup, then one might wonder where the red soup has come from. The red soup is supposed to be borscht, which is a beet soup with boiled vegetables, served with sour cream, boiled eggs or potatoes, and sometimes with dumplings. It is of Ukrainian origin commonly found in East European diets. Yet in Hong Kong nowadays, it is more common to find it as vegetable soup with beef bone stock, and the soup is served with bread before the main meal.

There are two routes of Western food in Hong Kong that are connected to two different kinds of soup served in local restaurants. Despite British and French influences, the second trend of Western food was introduced through Shanghai, with White Russian origins, and the major influx was probably in the 1950s. White Russians were defined as ethnic Russians living in the present region of Lithuania, Ukraine, and Latvia. Many of them left from the territory of former Imperial Russia after the Russian Revolution of 1917 (DeWolf 2017). They lived in Harbin, Beijing, and Shanghai, and some of them came to Hong Kong after China's liberation in 1949 and brought borscht (羅宋湯), beef stroganoff (俄式牛柳絲), and chicken kiev (雞卷), which were different from the Western dishes introduced through the Guangzhou area. I am not able to find detailed information about the relations between the White Russian people and Russian restaurants, except that some of the founding members of those restaurants might have been Russians. However, the presence of Shandong chefs who contributed to the operations including cooking and management should not be overlooked.

Some from the older generations might still remember Western restaurants such as Queen's (皇后), ABC (愛皮西), Cherikoff (車厘哥夫), Chantecler (雄雞), and Tkachenko,[1] even though most of them were closed in the 1990s. In an interview, DeWolf (2017) mentioned the kind of meals Russians had when growing up in Hong Kong:

> The daily menu for Chantecler, located on Hankow Road in Tsim Sha Tsui, began with a selection of zakouska (Russian hors d'oeuvres), followed by a bowl of borscht, fish meuniére with chips, and chicken à la king. Ice cream was served for dessert, along with coffee or tea.

The third Western food trend that arrived in Hong Kong was quite different from those with British or Russian influences, as it had less to do with the food but more with the services, especially the food and utensil arrangement in upscale Chinese restaurants. Today, if we attend a Chinese wedding banquet or enjoy formal Chinese set dinners in starred or recommended restaurants, the dishes will not be placed in the middle of a round table for sharing. Instead, an equal proportion of each item of the full course will be served individually on a white porcelain plate. This third trend, with the introduction of Western arrangement for Chinese food as well as what we used to call *nouvelle* Cantonese cuisine and its history, can be traced back to the economic development in Hong Kong in the late 1970s.

In Hong Kong, the emergence of *nouvelle* Cantonese cuisine served as an important indicator of the social construction of Hong Kong society. By the late 1970s, a visibly cosmopolitan Hong Kong with generations of Western-educated citizens were firmly in place.

Parallel to this post-war transformation, this modified Cantonese cuisine reflected how Hong Kong's social values were constructed. The transformation occurred in the form of *nouvelle*, or new, Cantonese cuisine in the late 1970s. The cuisine combined exotic or expensive ingredients with Western catering. The emergence of *nouvelle* Cantonese cuisine was first found in a host of tastefully decorated restaurants in Tsim Sha Tsui East. Other restaurants opened in areas such as Tsim Sha Tsui, Causeway Bay, and Central, and developed their own *nouvelle* Cantonese styles. This style of cuisine was characterized by exotic ingredients (such as peacock, crocodile, and kangaroo), new recipes (stewed in Western red wine), adventurous cooking techniques, excellent catering services (serving individual portions rather than family-style shared dishes, and changing dishes after each course of the meal), and outstanding décor and ambience. *Nouvelle* Cantonese cuisine was a taste deliberately created for and pursued by the 'new rich'. This process of culinary invention may reflect broad social and cultural trends: Hong Kong's increasingly wealthy and new middle class aspires for a lifestyle that is more glamorous and stresses greater refinement in the dining experience.

In the 1970s, Hong Kong's living standards had improved due to the city's economic achievements, and people were able to spend more on travelling and eating. Overseas tourism increased the demand for choices and distinctive forms of lifestyles. In addition, expectations for more delicate, exotic, and complicated food and cuisine were heightened. The demand for high quality lifeways as well as the development of individuals' taste can be seen through the emergence of *nouvelle* Cantonese cuisine that combines exotic taste, expensive ingredients, and Western catering. Goody (1982, 105) suggests that high cuisine refers to its characteristic: 'the higher in hierarchy, the wider the contacts, the broader the view', and that 'higher cuisine inevitably had to acquire ingredients from "outside"'. He draws our attention to the disparity between cuisine in terms of ingredients and technique within a context of global exchange. Changes in taste, cuisine, and eating habits are understood as social construction that is closely associated with the commodification of cultural objects used to express individual and group identities. It is not a surprise that foodways in Hong Kong back then became enormously diversified to serve different interests for expressing status, prestige, and power. Hong Kong's living standards improved with the increase in its economic achievements, and people were able to spend more on imported, brand-name products. They also travelled and dined out more often with their newfound wealth. For instance, the increase of overseas tourism heightened the demand for choice by local residents and for increased variety in distinctive modern city lifestyles. Likewise, this new wealth increased expectations for more delicate, exotic, and refined foods in the local diets.

In the summer of 2004, I was invited to co-host a fifteen-session, hourly radio programme called *Hong Kong Foodways*. It was produced by the government channel—Radio Television Hong Kong (RTHK). In the programme, I conducted interviews with famous chefs, restaurant owners, consultants, food critics, and experts. One of the guests for the programme was Ching, who is a prominent promoter of *nouvelle* Cantonese cuisine. Ching used to be an executive chef of a Chinese restaurant in a five-star hotel in Tsim Sha Tsui. He earned his high reputation after attending a Japanese television cooking show called *Iron Chef* (料理の鉄人 in Japanese). I was told that he was inspired by the fruits used by the Western restaurant in the same hotel he was working for, because they all looked very nice and exotic. Therefore, he ordered some for his Chinese dishes. Fruit is not a common ingredient in Chinese traditional dishes. Yet, Ching was successful and created one of his signature dishes—shark fin soup in Hawaiian papaya.

Until the 1980s, *nouvelle* Cantonese cuisine was popular because of the large demands from local elites, expatriates, and international visitors. However, in the late 1980s, many people migrated overseas. These included a lot of talented Chinese chefs who left Hong Kong for Cantonese restaurants in the United States, Canada, and Australia. While it might be true that the decline of *nouvelle* Cantonese cuisine was mainly caused by the migration wave at that time, the incoming international cuisines also played a competitive role in the upscale restaurant market. In addition, individual taste has continuously changed in the existing consumer society, and ways of mixing, combining, prioritizing, and reinventing became indicators of expected identity and status. The emergence of a style that emphasizes *freedom of choice* is a possible approach when examining the changing 'taste' of Hong Kong people in the last few decades.

For further discussion on the varieties of international cuisines found in the 1980s, I will compare Hong Kong eating habits inside the home with those outside, which clearly show some indicative differences. When people dine out, they seek variety and a wide range of choices. They perhaps eat in McDonald's for breakfast, lunch at a Japanese sushi restaurant, buy snacks at the Taiwan tea shop, and enjoy Indian curry for dinner. They might be eager to try Korean barbecue after having raw oysters from France as appetizers and Boston lobster from the United States. These different dishes from all over the world can be found easily in Hong Kong nowadays, and they are available to most people, not just the rich. However, food consumed inside the home is much more traditional and conservative, with concerns for safety, health, traditional hot/cold balance, and ritual taboos. A cultural boundary is maintained and well defined between eating at home and outside. Nevertheless, this negotiation between traditionalism and globalism in relation to domestic issues can be wholly observed in Hong Kong. The ingredients used in most Hong Kong homestyle cooking are highly similar and seldom vary. For example, boiled soup, steamed fish, fried seasonal green vegetables with small pieces of meat, and bean curd are all typical family dishes. Rice is almost always served. The difference between eating habits inside and outside the home is a telling one and reflects the dichotomy of Hong Kong itself. Hong Kong is a cosmopolitan city boasting international sophistication on the one hand, while on the other it is an extension of Chinese culture with long-standing Cantonese traditions. We can see some parallels that have developed since the emergence of *nouvelle* Cantonese cuisine in the 1970s, where different foods, such as American fast-food chains, French fine dining, Italian pasta, Japanese sushi, Korean barbeque, Thai spicy food, Vietnamese dishes, and other regional cuisines of China have continued to arrive and have significantly influenced Hong Kong in terms of foodways. Among all the non-Chinese dishes, Thai and Indian foods might have followed slightly different paths of development, as the Thai and Indian communities have their anchored neighbourhoods in Kowloon City and Tsim Sha Tsui. The restaurants and groceries found in these neighbourhoods are much like the Shanghainese model (see Chapter 2). To understand how non-Chinese food has contributed to the development of Hong Kong foodways, it is beneficial to look at the recent transformation of Hong Kong's Japanese food and, in particular, how it is different from other imported Western foodways that were brought to Hong Kong before and after the Second World War.

I grew up in Hong Kong with Cantonese parents from Chaozhou and Shunde, so Cantonese food was served at home most of the time. Non-Cantonese food was not unfamiliar, although there was no way for me to make a good comparison with anything outside Hong Kong. With limited knowledge of worldwide foodways, I went to Japan for tertiary education in 1984 when Japanese food was not widely known in Hong Kong except for *teppanyaki* (鉄板焼き in Japanese). The dish was featured prominently in a popular movie called *Teppanyaki*, directed by Michael Hui in 1984. In the film, the characters made fun of the skills of a *teppanyaki* chef. Not knowing the success story of Benihana[2] or cowboy-style grilled steak and seafood in the United States, many Hong Kong people (including myself) just thought that *teppanyaki* was an authentic as well as traditional way of serving beef steak and seafood in most Japanese restaurants.

My first *sashimi* (sliced raw fish) meal in Japan was a treat. The meal was a set lunch with five or six pieces of red tuna served with rice and miso soup. It was quite expensive to eat in the traditional sushi bar, and that would not be a common eating place for college students. Yet, around the same time, there was a rapid growth of modern sushi bars in Japan. These bars featured conveyor belt sushi (迴轉壽司), which had been invented in Osaka in 1958 and became widely popular in the 1980s. In such a bar, two pieces of the same sushi were put on a conveyor belt mounted on the bar. The sushi was on a plate with a specific colour that identified their price. Customers could pick the ones they liked without having to order in advance. Compared with traditional sushi places, these bars were cheap, and customers did not necessarily have to be familiar with the food. At that time, conveyor belt sushi was also seen as a trial for curious and adventurous Hong Kong consumers, since eating raw sliced fish and seafood was uncommon in their conventional diets.

When I returned from Japan in the mid-1990s, the number of Japanese eateries had increased and they were not limited to *teppanyaki*. There were places that also served sushi, tempura, and other traditional Japanese food. Apart from the traditional dishes served in upscale restaurants, the number of B-class gourmets (such as ramen, curry, and deep-fried pork chop), which have been popular in Japan since the 1990s, increased after the Japan economic bubble burst and began to change the landscape of Japanese food in Hong Kong as well (Ng 2006). There were more ramen (noodles) shops and conveyor belt sushi available in many neighbourhoods. And since the last two decades, there has been a prominent increase of restaurants that specialize in different kinds of regional ramen, curries, and pork cutlet (*tonkatsu*). There are also fast food chains for Japanese burgers, restaurants that serve Japanese-style pasta and pizza, steak houses, whisky bars, cake shops, and cafés. During the COVID-19 pandemic in 2020–2021, a Japanese supermarket opened a few branches in downtown areas with most food items imported directly from Japan. There is a Japanese niche for all those eateries and shops that have become popular and trustworthy among Hong Kong people. There are multiple reasons behind this phenomenon. Apart from a good variety of regional food products promoted through domestic and international tourism, the formalization of food appreciation through anime, manga, TV series, and movies are also commonly seen as the rationale for their success and promotion of their soft power. In the context of globalizing Japanese popular culture, snacks and drinks such as *matcha* cookies, chocolate (with Japanese milk), Japanese cheesecake, Japanese whisky, sake (Japanese rice wine), *shochu* (liquor mainly made by sweet potatoes), and gin with specific Japanese herbs and flavourings can be found easily in Hong Kong.

Due to Japan's policy of promoting food overseas, Japanese beef, rice, and snacks have reached more consumers in many countries, and Hong Kong is no exception. 'Direct delivery' (產地直送) is often mentioned in Japanese restaurants, and the concept of *omakase* (i.e., literally meaning 'leave it up to you', commonly used at Japanese restaurants where the customer leaves it up to the chef for the choices of daily and seasonal specialties) has been well accepted by Hong Kong's Japanese food lovers. They completely trust the chef as well as the eatery. As mentioned earlier, Hong Kong people are willing to try different kinds of food and are adventurous to discover various cultures through eating and sharing. During the last few decades, in addition to the growing interest in Japanese food, European foodways have also become more visible. Spanish ham, Dutch seafood, wine, and confectioneries are popular among young professionals in Hong Kong. One of the reasons for their popularity is probably related to these young people's cultural experiences; they encounter people from all over the world and are willing to learn more about various cultures and lifestyles through foodways. The corresponding changes reflected by the rise and popularity of *nouvelle* Chinese and international foodways should not be overlooked, because they provide a channel for understanding how values and norms changed due to economic success and social stability, after the hard times of the 1960s that most people experienced.

In contrast to foodways brought by the incoming migrants in the post-war era, this chapter illustrates how technical changes such as logistics and modern ways of transport played another kind of important role in the changing foodways. The ideas of *nouvelle* cuisine and the popularization of Japanese food with its global export system are merely part of the changing modes and tastes in the larger picture of Hong Kong foodways.

In Chapter 4, in alignment with the concerns of local heritage and authentic traditional practices, which have become another popular food theme in real life and in the media since the 1990s, I would like to discuss the search for nostalgic food, with the emphasis on local and homestyle cooking.

# 4
# In Search of Nostalgic Food

In addition to the varieties of international cuisine we find in Hong Kong nowadays, there is a kind of food that individuals are emotionally attached to. If I had to name my comfort food, I would probably say claypot rice (煲仔飯) with steamed chicken/pork ribs and Chinese sausage (see Figure 4.1) and Cantonese congee cooked with preserved duck egg and lean pork meat (皮蛋瘦肉粥) (see Figure 4.2). Both can be found everywhere in Hong Kong. For the younger generations, street food is the comfort or nostalgic food of choice, while for those who are living away from their families, homemade soup is probably another popular choice. If the choice of comfort food is largely based on individual experiences, nostalgic food might have more to do with the social norms and values in the cultural and political context. For most people in Hong Kong, a few nostalgic food serving similar purposes can be identified.

Since the Hong Kong handover, Hakka tea dumplings (茶粿) have become popular among both Hakka people and urbanites. Most of the dumplings are homemade and sold by elderly ladies in old neighbourhoods and villages, and they offer a taste of authenticity and tradition. The most common type is made of glutinous rice flour and sugar and carries the flavour of *paederia foetida* (雞屎藤). Other

Figure 4.1: Claypot rice

Figure 4.2: Cantonese congee

flavours include *artemisia argyi* (艾草), sweet potato, and pumpkin. Given people's increasing interest in local traditions, Hakka dumplings might shed light on what nostalgic food looks like. Similarly, other Punti Hakka snacks such as glutinous rice wine, pop-rice bar, and seafood dishes made with local ingredients have been attracting more attention since the last two decades.

As mentioned earlier, one of the four groups of indigenous inhabitants in the New Territories were Punti Hakka. Their early influx was related to the evacuation order for the isolation of the anti-Qing movement on the coastal area from Shandong to Guangdong during the early Qing dynasty. Hakka people have since been officially brought to this area after the evacuation order was removed. Therefore, a large number of Hakka villagers in the north-eastern part of the New Territories claimed that their ancestors came in the Qing period and that they have a family history of more than 300 years. Even though they have settled in the New Territories for more than 300 years, they are still distinguished by their language, architecture, foodways, gender relations, and lifeways. Punti Hakka were the early settlers on the hilly lands of the eastern peninsula, while the Punti, also known as Wai Tsuen or Wai Tau people (圍村人 or 圍頭人), farmed the fertile lowland during the pre-colonial era. Therefore, villages located in areas such as Sha Tau Kok, Hang Hau Peninsula, Tai Mo Shan, Tai Po, Shatin, Tsuen Wan, Tsing Yi, and Ma Wan were commonly identified as Punti Hakka villages.

As these Hakka people came from a coastal environment, it is not surprising to see how their dietary practices changed accordingly. The emphasis on freshness while cooking seafood and their excessive use of dried marine products is highly noticeable. My observations of a few Punti Hakka dishes that are commonly served in a few restaurants are as follows: (1) fish (eel) maw with minced pork, dried shrimp, and squash in soup (勝瓜蝦米肉碎煮魚鰾; dried marine products are used for traditional festive food; it is a signature dish for the New Year family banquet) (see Figure 4.3); (2) salty water chicken/duck/goose (鹹雞/鴨/鵝; emphasis is placed on freshness; the dish is obviously different from that of the salty baked style with sand ginger, which is served in other Hakka restaurants discussed in Chapter 2); and (3) stewed pork with black fungi and large squid (大墨魚木耳炆豬肉; dried fungi and seafood instead of pickled vegetable [see Figure 4.4]; also, only the kind of squids that come back to the coastal area in the early spring are used). The preparation of these dishes is more time-consuming and depends on the supply of local seasonal ingredients that must be freshly caught or harvested. Therefore, not many restaurants serve these dishes. However, these are delicacies that the nostalgic food followers enjoy.

As for the nostalgic food in Hong Kong, I would like to introduce a few that I categorize as *low (everyday) cuisine*. These include traditional village food and homestyle eating venues. This kind of cuisine might help us understand how local residents have reacted to the cultural, economic, and political changes and refashioned their identities in post-handover Hong Kong. Investigating the consumption of such low cuisine that encompasses specific regional characteristics, methods of domestic service, and local southern Chinese ingredients shows how people use their traditional roots to craft meaning vis-à-vis *haute*/high cuisine, which emphasizes the use of exotic (often imported or rare) and expensive ingredients, cooking techniques, and professional high-end service that are globally recognized. The subsequent commercialization of the low cuisine in the post-handover Hong Kong highlights how this aspect of material culture moves across diverse cultural practices and redefines its meanings, and how the marginal, rural, daily, and common foodways have played upon people's nostalgia for tradition, remembrance of the past, and an imagination of the *good old days*.

**Figure 4.3:** Fish maw soup cooked with dried shrimp, minced pork, and gourd

**Figure 4.4:** Hakka stewed pork

Before discussing the nature and history of two kinds of the low cuisine—*puhn choi* (盆菜, or basin food) and *si fohng choi* (私房菜, or private kitchen food)—it is important to look at the post-war Hakka restaurants which had witnessed Hong Kong's industrial development (see Chapter 2). These restaurants still bring back a lot of good memories for the older generations. Travel in mainland China became more popular among Hong Kong people, and traditional architecture and vernacular village settlements became prominent tourist destinations after the 1997 handover. Traditional local foodways provided a taste of nostalgia and a localized cultural identity desired by heritage-seeking tourists. I investigated this popular trend of embracing low cuisine as part of the social and political changes after the handover of Hong Kong to the People's Republic of China (PRC) in 1997.[1] Following the handover, people in Hong Kong continued to express very mixed feelings about this 'return' of sovereignty. Part of this ambiguity stems from questions of what it means to be 'Hongkongese' and who is 'Chinese'—a controversial issue that continues to be debated and contested (Lau and Kuan 1988). Is one's identity, and thus one's shared sociocultural background, rooted in one's place of birth, such as the Pearl River Delta, where ancestors of most Hong Kong people had come from? On the one hand, Hong Kong residents share a few similarities in their sense of identity such as language, religion, and food. On the other hand, there are local-born, Western-educated, young professionals who consider themselves Hongkongese. There are also established immigrant businessmen who consider themselves Chinese, and many who feel that they fall between the two. Thus, a sense of belonging in Hong Kong is not homogeneous and has never been solidly achieved across all sectors of society. The changing dynamics of food and cuisine, and the consumption of low cuisine with the emphasis on local and homestyle cooking, provide an entry point for understanding how different people identify themselves and their place in society with such dramatic social and political change.

The well-known country-style dish *puhn choi* (basin food) is a festive food commonly prepared for ancestral worship rites and wedding banquets. The dish is popular among the Punti indigenous inhabitants of the New Territories (see Figure 4.5) and is usually prepared in the kitchen of the ancestral hall. It is the main and only dish served. All ingredients are served in one basin, or *puhn*, from which people at the table eat communally. This dish usually comprises layers of inexpensive, local ingredients such as dried pig skin, dried eel, dried squid, radish, tofu skin, mushroom, and pork stewed in soybean paste. Several other dishes may occasionally be included in a banquet, but the basin dish is always the focus. Among local villagers in the New Territories, the dish is usually called *sihk puhn* (食盆; literally means 'eat the basin') and boasts an oral history longer than that of colonial Hong Kong. Most importantly, *sihk puhn*'s contemporary manifestation as *puhn choi* is promoted in the media (e.g., guidebooks, websites, and travel magazines) through different stories of its so-called origin. Yet, the tradition of eating *puhn choi* in Hong Kong appears to have attracted domestic tourists only after their visits to the region's traditional village settlements and heritage sites in the New Territories (visits to the latter have become more common since the 1990s).

Because of these legendary, albeit constructed, origins, *puhn choi* is currently considered a re-invented, regional country-style food that represents cultural traditions and the local uniqueness of a lineage-oriented social structure in the New Territories. There are many different versions of *puhn choi*'s origin. For example, it has been said that *puhn choi* began as leftovers from a village banquet and was highly appreciated by Qing Emperor Ch'ien Lung (Qianlong, 乾隆) when he was visiting Kwangtung (Guangdong) (Watson 1987, 394). Another two popular versions related to the Southern Song dynasty say that *puhn*

**Figure 4.5:** *Puhn choi*

*choi* was originally the food given to the Song Emperor Zhao Bing (趙昺) and his entourage, and Wen Tianxiang (文天祥), who was a poet and a politician. Interestingly, both men in those stories emphasized the moment when they moved to the south during the invasion of the Mongolians in the late Song period. The dish was later named *puhn choi* because there were not enough containers to hold food for everyone, so washing basins used by villagers became the containers for the army's feast (Tang 2002, 4). These stories thus reflect the historical consciousness of the state from a local perspective.

*Puhn choi* functions as a local foodway for Chinese family lineages settled in the New Territories several centuries ago, and speaks of the exotic for most Hong Kong residents who are not familiar with cultural traditions in the area. *Puhn choi*'s double identity—both local and exotic—has been promoted widely in domestic tourism for its 'taste of tradition'. Domestic tours and popular package tours generally include local food (usually *puhn choi*, seafood, or a vegetarian meal), rural scenery, and a visit to historic pre-colonial villages or temples to reinforce the image of a traditional Hong Kong. Visiting the rural part of the New Territories is, for urban Hong Kong residents, a journey into their inner selves. This search for a Hong Kong tradition reflects the identity awareness or crisis felt by Hong Kong residents before the handover in 1997.

My first encounter with *puhn choi* was in 1995 when I visited the newly established Ping Shan Heritage Trail in Yuen Long with a group of anthropology students. After the visit, we went to a casually constructed restaurant that served only *puhn choi* for tourists. We decided to try because there was no other choice, and we also thought it was a suitable experience after understanding the culture and history of the traditional settlements in Ping Shan. That was my first *puhn choi* meal and I did not have any knowledge of the dish before this. I was surprised to see all the ingredients served in a big Chinese porcelain container/basin which was placed in the middle of a round table for a total of ten to twelve people. Hong Kong urbanites might have tasted country-style cooking before, but the dish became more widely known when people joined the popular local one-day tours (本地一日遊) to the New Territories.

In addition to history-inspired village traditions, steady forward-looking infrastructure developments in the New Territories also contributed to the sharp increase in demand for *puhn choi* in Hong Kong. Duruz (2001) similarly observes in Australia that the history of certain traditional foods is significantly anchored in politics and a nationalistic ideology that valorizes earlier eras. Duruz argues that a main determining force in what people expect from so-called traditional foods is a feeling of nostalgia as well as a cultural identification with the past through eating in the present. This may explain why *puhn choi* has become so popular since the 1990s. Convenient transportation facilitates travel, and therefore people can more easily experience the rural traditions in the New Territories, a region that was considered remote until the 1980s. However, the change from eating the traditional *sihk puhn* (eat the basin) to the modern *puhn choi* (basin cuisine) needs further examination. Historically speaking, *sihk puhn* has been served as banquet food in many local, single-surname villages. The dish marks corresponding ethnic boundaries and is ceremonially used to signify an entire lineage that is joined by the way they eat together. As Watson (1987) points out, the practice of *sihk puhn* is an indicator of equality and commonness among the lineage members, and their disregard of status and social achievements. Watson (1987, 391–392) states that:

> [e]ach quest collected his own chopsticks from a tray and picked up an individual bowl of steamed rice. The basin was carried to an unoccupied corner of the hall. Earlier arrivals were already eating at the few makeshift tables that had been assembled near the kitchen. I could not help but notice that one of the wealthiest men in rural Hong Kong (an emigrate millionaire) was sitting between a retired farmer and a factory worker . . . No ceremonies of any kind were performed, no complicated codes of etiquette were observed. No one acted as host for our small group and there was no ranking of diners, nor was there a head table reserved for important guests. People were fed on a first come, first served basis. No speeches were delivered and no toasts proposed. Everyone ate at their own place and left when they pleased.

*Sihk puhn* not only reinforces the *punti* (local) single-surname lineage system but also seems to exclude Hakka groups from punti Chinese groups within the political context of the New Territories. In other words, *sihk puhn* is metaphorically regarded as the real food of the New

Territories, which dates back to the period when the first inhabitants settled in the area (Watson 1987).

In the early 1990s, Hong Kong urbanites who participated in these *discovery voyages* of the local and domestic traditions in the New Territories and their affiliated expectations of exoticism did so, in part, to reassert their Hongkongness within the context of identity crisis involved in the 1997 handover. On the one hand, *puhn choi*, with an emphasis on local tradition, represented a kind of exotic element in the promotion of domestic tourism. On the other hand, it developed as a metaphor for Hong Kong people's search for a sense of cultural belonging at the end of the British rule in Hong Kong. *Puhn choi* now carried a political message and moved from its original function as a focus for lineage gathering in the New Territories to a symbol of Hong Kong heritage that anyone could share.

Apart from being served the traditional way, *takeaway puhn choi* in a large bowl for ten to twelve people is also popular. Thus, one can enjoy this dish with friends and relatives at home instead of traditional venues such as village halls or cemeteries for festive and ceremonial occasions. Most interestingly, during the Lunar New Year holidays in 2003, it was widely reported in the media that *puhn choi* was one of the bestsellers despite the economic depression. Many takeaway *puhn choi* meals were sold on the second day of the Lunar New Year; traditionally, the first family meal of the year is served on the second day of the new year, and all family members are in attendance. In the following two decades, the demand for *puhn choi* remained consistent, and some versions of this dish were served and sold (as takeaway) in high-end seafood restaurants. Its popularity and unfamiliarity are well reflected by the fact that the Hong Kong government wrote a press release to outline the facts that people should note when purchasing and preparing *puhn choi* during the Lunar New Year of 2005 (HKSARG 2005a; 2005b). In January 2005, the most popular local Chinese-language food magazine at the time—*Eat & Travel Weekly*—published a special issue on the varieties of *puhn choi*, ranging from traditional meals prepared in ancestral halls to expensive meals with fresh seafood or dried marine products. And there was still another variation—miniature *puhn choi*. This mini version uses a small pumpkin as the basin and the ingredients include a few pieces of chicken, mushrooms, and vegetables. It was actively promoted by some local fast-food chains and was served in single portions as well as a single dinner set. As *puhn choi* conveys an image of family meals and symbolizes *Hongkongness*, the dish has entered Hong Kong's daily life in multiple ways (S. Chan 2010; K. S. Chan 2011).

In the 2004 radio programme I mentioned earlier, one of the guests on the show was Wing, who is a prominent promoter of country-style food and the New Territories village food. His restaurant was successful in serving dishes developed from the traditional *puhn choi* and in bringing different local homestyle food into the commercial sphere. Apart from being a renowned chef, Wing is famous for his television show and enjoys the reputation of knowing where good food can be found. In his television show, viewers follow Wing on his travels to locate high quality ingredients. Unlike other popular food critics in the media, Wing does not emphasize the use of luxurious, high-end, expensive meals, but focuses on Cantonese traditional country food prepared with care. In the programme, he discusses the differences between good and bad ingredients and how, during cooking, one can make full use of local food's tastes, textures, and characteristics. From December 2002 to July 2003, Wing published four books on traditional food. The first one is a cookbook on village (or *wai tsuen*) food in the New Territories; the second is about eating in the Pearl River Delta area; the third and fourth are cookbooks that include the history of traditional sauces along with hints for choosing ingredients and culinary techniques compiled after a popular television series on looking for good food in the Pearl River Delta area. Between August

2003 and July 2004, Wing published three more books with similar themes. These books not only showcase simple cooking methods with local ingredients, but also reinforce how everyday material culture has assumed centre stage in a transformed cultural practice of the time. In addition to the recipes and illustrations of the dishes, Wing also describes some of his personal experiences through which he learned of those dishes. He always reminds his readers of the close relationship between local ingredients and their environment.

I think that locally situated foods such as *puhn choi* and television programmes and books that focus on the production of local food in different parts of the Pearl River Delta area, including Hong Kong, help raise the audience's consciousness to the source of the food but also their Chinese roots through the discovery of foodways. As to the complex relations between food and memory, Sutton (2001, 161) suggests that the investigation of food and eating can assist in understanding how past recollections construct an imagined tradition and identity. These food voyages materialize an identity of Hong Kong heritage through eating habits, linking Hong Kong to the mainland territories and an imagined past, rather than isolating Hong Kong from this historical connection within the wave of global capital. Television programmes, such as the one hosted by Wing, present their audiences with an imagined Chinese identity. Apart from food demonstrations and in-kitchen country-style and nostalgic cooking shows, the so-called traditional foodways also help promote awareness of one's heritage and a sense of cultural belonging by making the 'roots' of Hong Kong people's eating habits visible. In so doing, they enforce for viewers a cultural identity to the Pearl River Delta area, an imagined *homeland*.

Private kitchen food (私房菜) is regarded as another renowned example of low cuisine. It demonstrates, like *puhn choi*, how material culture can move from the margins to the centre of Hong Kong foodways. Private kitchens, in contrast with restaurants open to public customers, had no formal eatery licence in the 1990s when they first became popular, and some of them were run in residential apartments. The term 'private kitchen food' clearly highlights and identifies this sphere of cuisine with the places in which homemade food is prepared. Further, the term emphasizes that these dishes comprise homestyle cooking prepared by specific chefs or with characteristics that recall domesticity. During the mid-1990s, when *puhn choi* was increasingly popular, private kitchens also became one of the trendiest types of eateries in Hong Kong. There were more than two hundred private kitchens at their peak. These establishments have since gained more popularity among Hong Kong residents and foreign visitors and have attracted the attention of major guidebook publishers and overseas presses (Simonds 2004; Sterling, Chong, and Qin 2001, 148). For example, there are Chinese eateries, such as Mum Chau's Sichuan Kitchen, Da Ping Huo, Yellow Door, Chow Chung, Shanghai Delight, and Secret Pantry; and Western eateries, such as Plats, Gio's, La Bouteille, Chez Copains, LIPS, and Bo Inno Seki. Each of these home-kitchen restaurants places a strong emphasis on unconventional Cantonese Chinese, European homestyle cooking, or fusion food. For example, a report in the *South China Morning Post* (Hong Kong's major English-language newspaper) heralded private kitchens as the newest form of localized eatery:

> World Food Hong Kong describes private kitchen[s] as "speakeasies," a term from the 1920s Prohibition era in the US when alcohol sales were banned and drinkers met in illegal clubs … [the] owner of a successful operation called Shanghai Delight, says private kitchens are more of an art than a business. "We are selling our identity—it's in the decoration, the menu, and the cooking. We are sharing our own experience of our Chinese food culture openly with others." (Chan 2003a)

In Hong Kong, earlier private kitchens are unlicenced restaurants identified as exclusive eating places by the middle class. They are still generally places with no registered company name and located in residential and industrial/factory buildings. There are no walk-in customers, and reservations need to be made, sometimes more than one month in advance. There are no menus because the food to be served is determined by the owners. There is no service charge, and no credit cards are accepted. Some private kitchens advertise their prices, menus, and locations on their websites. Prices for a meal range from HK$500 to $800 (US$60 to US$100). It is not considered inexpensive when compared with other restaurants that serve similar food. In terms of location, nowadays besides those that serve food in the chef's home, most of them are in factory buildings in old industrial neighbourhoods where rental fees are relatively low. The majority of the private kitchens often serve only dinner, and some open only a few days each week. The interior décor is usually simple, but attempts are made to recreate an ambience of home, albeit artistic in nature, due, in part, to the fact that some owners and promoters of the private kitchens are practising artists. The domestic atmosphere is created by using dim or soft lighting and stylish rather than industrial furniture, reflecting the individual taste of the owner.

Because of such underground and seemingly exclusive operations, as well as their culinary techniques promoted as homestyle cooking, food offered in these private kitchens carries an image of comfort and *hominess*. Most of the customers come from the middle class. Occasionally, celebrities and artists, who are attracted by both the homemade food setting and the distinctive personalities of the hosts and/or owners, visit too. Although a number of these private kitchens had ceased their operations by 2004, I estimate that more than one hundred of these eateries remain in Hong Kong. While some still try to maintain their underground image in terms of services and the character of homemade food, many have been converted from underground (as well as illegal) operations to formal licenced restaurants. Thus, the manufacture of non-Cantonese dishes into homestyle food, the explanation of the unlicenced as private, and the image of being underground yet user-friendly and even tourist-friendly demonstrate how homestyle cooking can be packaged, marketed, and accepted by local and Asian visitors. This is evidenced in a timely column in the *South China Morning Post*. The story reports that Japanese and Southeast Asian visitors, in search of an authentic local Hong Kong dining experience, found their way to private kitchens after seeing different promotions in the media. One of the restaurant owners explains, '[M]any tourists dined at [the] French private kitchen, La Bouteille, after it was featured in a Japanese airline in-flight magazine and in a Japanese TV documentary program' (Chan 2003b).

One of the earliest private kitchens, for example, established in the late 1990s by a Sichuan couple, is famous for its homestyle renditions of locally rooted Sichuan food. The husband, who is also a painter, designed the interior, and the wife, a singer, is the chef. When the restaurant was first opened, it operated only three days a week. These days, it has expanded its business hours to serve dinner nightly. However, the restaurant still does not display a sign outside the entrance, and the owners do not advertise in any way. The restaurant has gained its reputation solely by word of mouth. To augment the restaurant's personal touch, the owner has decorated the interior with his paintings, each of which combines Western and Chinese artistic techniques and motifs. The restaurant seats up to sixty people (six tables for two to ten persons), and there are two sittings per night, starting at 6:30 p.m. and 9:15 p.m. Following the meal, the chef performs a song to the customers-audience to express her gratitude as the host. To secure dinner reservations from last-minute cancellations, the restaurant owners require a deposit of 50 per cent of the approximate value of the meal at least three days in advance of the reservation. Such expectations highlight the middle- to upper-middle-class status of the regular clientele and the allure of the restaurant's fare, which was previously considered local and lower class. The owners emphasize their ongoing practice of avoiding 'fancy dishes' but serve, instead, dishes that recall traditional and homestyle Sichuan food. Here, then, food moves across diverse cultural spheres of meaning, making the local simultaneously exotic and familiar for adventure-seeking consumers.

Another Sichuan private kitchen, established in 2000, is famous for its homemade dumplings, noodles, and various kinds of spicy dishes. The owner is not a professional chef by training, nor is he an artist. However, he achieves fame and immediate recognition through the delicious and innovative Sichuan country food he makes for his clients and friends. This restaurant, like the one noted earlier, is in an older historical building. Its decoration is simple. There are only a few pictures of the owner's hometown and several calligraphies are hanging on the wall. Some typical items on the restaurant's menu include dumplings, stewed pork, green vegetables stir-fried with salted pork, spicy noodles, free-range chicken dishes, and plain fried sweet corn. Just like other private kitchens serving Sichuanese, Hunan, Shanghainese, traditional Cantonese, and Hakka dishes, such dining fare clearly illustrates that these establishments showcase low cuisine with an emphasis on rural, country, and homestyle food presented in personalized, warm, and home-like settings.

Besides non-Cantonese regional cuisines, some private kitchens serve Cantonese-origin fusion food. A comparatively new private kitchen of this kind is aptly located in the older neighbourhood of Sheung Wan or the South–North Corridor, a district that includes both commercial and residential areas and is home to the wholesale trade of dried marine/fish products and Chinese herbal medicine. This private kitchen is operated by a chef who is well known in Japan. He became widely known because of his participation in the popular Japanese television programme *Iron Chef*. The restaurant serves his unique version of homestyle Cantonese fusion food. He explains that, since his retirement from a Chinese restaurant in a Hong Kong five-star hotel, his former customers, as well as his friends, continually encouraged him to open a private kitchen so that they could continue to enjoy his Cantonese fusion food. While this chef has pushed the parameters of *low* cuisine by combining multiple ingredients that do not all hail from local roots, he insists that he is recreating domestic-style food, as he is situating the food within a Hong Kong home environment. He grounds the rationale for his service in personalized and attentive relations with clients to make them 'feel as if they were dining at home'. In addition, the fact that his restaurant functions as an underground and exclusive eatery, not only for local people, but also for expatriates and international visitors (in particular, Japanese nationals living in Hong Kong), testifies to the allure of the domestic setting that provides an authentic Hong Kong home experience.

In Hong Kong, private kitchens do not have a direct historical precedent, although some food writers have suggested to me that the concept of private kitchens can be traced back to a type of highly exclusive private clubs developed during the 1960s. Frequented primarily by bankers and traders, these clubs were renowned for serving such unique local delicacies as snake soup. Here, we have a different kind of private kitchen that represents a contemporary conflation of the everyday, homemade food people eat but with a commercialized rendition and image of home. There is no surprise that expatriates and visitors are attracted to private kitchens, but one might wonder why the local middle class is interested in private kitchens as well. In fact, we have to be aware that the migrants who grew up in Hong Kong do not know much about their parents' home places, and most of them are not interested in learning about the lifestyles in which their parents were brought up. This also extends to foodways. According to my daily observations, local culinary skills are no longer passed down from parents to their children. The younger generations in Hong Kong, for example, do not often prepare or cook traditional festive foods at home, such as Lunar New Year snacks and seasonal specialties. In many middle-class families, cooking is done by immigrant domestic helpers, so the idea of homestyle cooking and traditional domestic food is often based on an imagined domesticity constructed by television dramas, movies, advertisements, and urban myths, instead of actual life experiences. A commercial setup conveying a warm and cosy atmosphere, family management and homemade food, and a residential environment and private location give a promising illusion of home for which customers are willing to pay.

Considering their rather short history in Hong Kong, private kitchens are still undergoing substantial changes as their popularity, at times, fluctuates. The first Sichuan kitchen that I mentioned earlier is no longer as busy as it was initially. My conversations with clients reveal that throughout 2004, the restaurant was seldom fully booked and that one could obtain a reservation at the last moment. The owner of the second Sichuan kitchen told me that he was also serving dinners to large tour groups from the Mainland, and most current customers of the third newly established private kitchen are Japanese rather than local Hong Kong people. Despite the decline in the number of private kitchens in 2004, the sharp rise in their popularity following the handover of Hong Kong demonstrates people's nostalgia for an 'old' Hong Kong, one that was partially rooted in the tradition of the Mainland.

The emergence of private kitchens, then, draws our attention to questions of ambiguity. These establishments gained popularity by providing so-called authentic Chinese regional cuisine, but in exclusive and underground environments. After the 1997 handover, Hong Kong residents puzzled over how they wanted to position themselves vis-à-vis their identity and their engagement with the Mainland. Were they Chinese or Hongkongese? People realized that the new political alliance opened new markets for mainland Chinese traders in Hong Kong; at the same time, it also provided more far-reaching opportunities for Hong Kong professionals in China. Many local and Western-educated, middle-class youth claim that they have not yet fully resolved the questions linked to their Chinese identity, given the recent political transformation. In the case study here, I observe that a *homey* private kitchen functions as a metaphor for belonging, although it is an ambiguous one. It is not the experience of home for most Cantonese living in Hong Kong, because private kitchens are commercialized, and the food is mostly spicy and exotic non-Cantonese food. However, eating at a private kitchen is an easy way for Hong Kong residents to take a brief voyage to China—a stepping stone to safely explore a Mainland way of life. More importantly, diners can enjoy the experience with friends who share similar concerns.

Why, then, did such everyday, mundane food become so popular? And with its increased demand, how did its subsequent commercialization affect its association with eating regional/provincial, domestic, and nostalgic food to construct a new identity in the transition from pre- to post-handover Hong Kong? Low cuisine refers to the preparation and consumption of inexpensive, ordinary, and local homestyle food, as opposed to *haute*/high cuisine with expensive, exotic, and imported ingredients served in a *classy*, fine-dining atmosphere. In this book, low cuisine also refers to commercialized regional, domestic, and nostalgic food; these foods are neither prepared by people with professional culinary skills, nor are they served through labour-intensive catering services. Low cuisine is prepared simply and served and eaten daily in Hong Kong neighbourhoods. The commercialization and commoditization of the tastes and practice of *country-style cooking, mom's cooking*, homemade food, or traditional cooking inevitably raise the issue of authenticity. As Handler (1986, 2) suggests, 'authenticity is a cultural construct closely tied to Western notions of the individual' rather than any notion implicit in non-Western societies such as China. My analysis, here, focuses on questions regarding the social and cultural implications of the popularity of low cuisine, the construction of Hongkongeseness, and the phenomenon of searching for local identity and a sense of cultural belonging in a commoditized world. As most low cuisine dishes are prepared differently each time they are made (different venues, different chefs, and different ingredients), the ways in which people consider them *authentic* are always rooted in varied local cultural meanings.

Considering the rapid development of Hong Kong and the Mainland, this transitional function of the private kitchens was rather short-lived and, indeed, the concept of these exclusive yet everyday institutions has changed in the last two decades. I would also argue that the earlier transitional function of private kitchens has currently been adopted and further developed by new restaurants that focus on regional and provincial cuisine. In 2004, in addition to the revival of Hakka and Shunde cuisines in these emerging restaurants in downtown areas, Beijing-Sichuan-Shanghai food chains also opened in major shopping malls and in New Town areas. People's interest in these local cuisines, initiated by the earlier private kitchens, has thus set the stage for the current popularity of eating establishments that feature regional cuisines (with an emphasis on country-style cooking). The number of these restaurants has grown in Hong Kong during the last decade. Apart from their development in Hong Kong since the 1990s, it is interesting to see how the concept of private kitchens will exert influence on mainland China. The concern about local ingredients and culinary skills inherited from family members have brought people to appreciate the food. Regional traditions and history have also made people feel proud of talking about their stories with friends and in the social media. In

Hong Kong, the nature of private kitchens may have changed, but the continuing popularity of private kitchens is still significant. For example, chefs are cooking in special pop-up venues. Meanwhile, more private kitchens are operating in renovated industrial buildings, and instead of regional Chinese cuisines, more are serving Western dishes with free corkage to attract wine drinkers.

# 5
# The Awareness of Food Heritage

While traditional food items may have been used for survival and to keep families alive, commercialization has discredited their authenticity from the perspective of preservation. In Hong Kong, we know that we are not going to bring back life foodways from the past, which have not been cooked or eaten in modern times. Yet we still face the dilemma of preserving traditional foodways that have been modified for market interests or paying more attention to hybridized foodways that are highly popular and commercially sustained. This makes us consider how to evaluate intangible heritage that has undergone transformation for the sake of survival. According to the UNESCO 2003 *Convention for the Safeguarding of the Intangible Cultural Heritage*, intangible cultural heritage is defined as:

> [T]he practices, representations, expressions, knowledge, skills—as well as the instruments, objects, artefacts, and cultural spaces associated therewith—that communities, groups and, in some cases, individuals recognize as part of their cultural heritage. This intangible cultural heritage, transmitted from generation to generation, is constantly recreated by communities and groups in response to their environment, their interaction with nature and their history, and provides them with a sense

of identity and continuity, thus promoting respect for cultural diversity and human creativity. (UNESCO 2003, 4)

Five domains of cultural heritage are listed: 'oral traditions and expressions, including language as a vehicle of the intangible cultural heritage; performing arts; social practices, rituals, and festive events; knowledge and practices concerning nature and the universe; and traditional craftsmanship' with the obligations on the state to put efforts into preservation processes (UNESCO 2003), and has a strong emphasis upon:

> [the] processes of globalization and social transformation, alongside the conditions they create for renewed dialogue among communities, also give rise, as does the phenomenon of intolerance, to grave threats of deterioration, disappearance and destruction of the intangible cultural heritage, in particular owing to a lack of resources for safeguarding such heritage. (UNESCO 2003, 1)

There is no doubt that many countries have attempted to get their foodways listed on UNESCO's Representative List of the Intangible Cultural Heritage of Humanity. For instance, French gastronomic meals and traditional Mexican cuisines were listed in 2010 respectively. Making and sharing kimjang as well as kimchi (泡菜製作及分享) from both South Korea (2013) and North Korea (2015), transnational submissions such as the Mediterranean Diet (2013), Washoku (和食) from Japan (2013), and hawker culture in Singapore (2020) have all been successfully listed. From 2010 to 2020, there were altogether twenty-two food-related items listed and they were linked to thirty-two countries. For individual countries, whether they are UNESCO members or not, there is no doubt that various food-related practices have been recognized and promoted as both regional and national cultures. Apart from these champion examples that represent relevant national cultures, there are many more food-related cases with similar concerns that we might have neglected.

We may never find the right moment for intangible heritage preservation. In other words, we are either too late to rescue the extinguished items or too early to include modified or commercialized items for preservation. Thus, it is important that we should try to pass down traditional foodways to the next generation, and yet we also have to accept that some of these traditions have already undergone transformations due to commercial interest and might have already, or mostly, disappeared. And I am sure Hong Kong is not an exception.

Among the 480 items listed as Hong Kong intangible cultural heritage (ICH), there are a good number of food or food-related items, such as the techniques for making bean curd, soy sauce, milk tea, *ying yang* (a mixed drink with tea and coffee), egg tart, and pineapple bun, along with *sihk puhn*, sweet potato cake, herbal tea, oyster cultivation, and fishing methods. I think these are all important for the understanding of our history and culture and could be recognized as ICH.

However, I think we also need to establish certain global values, instead of placing so much significance on local traditions. Just like the hawker culture in Singapore, we might want to consider the tea café (茶餐廳) as a total concept, instead of an eatery that serves a list of items. We might want to emphasize its inclusive atmosphere for people of different classes, ages, gender, and social status, and the diversity of dishes that the tea café serves. These dishes are with characteristics from many places and specially adapted in terms of forms and taste. Before giving further critical views on the existing ICH list, I would like to discuss the differences between culture and heritage. Making use of Hakka food for comparison, I argue that the post-war Hakka food served for the working class should be part of the Hong Kong culture because it has been part of the city's substantial eating habits since the

1950s. Hakka food reflects not only the dietary practices but also social values and relationships. However, I consider the Punti Hakka food a significant part of the intangible cultural heritage because it has evolved from a specific environment and has been developed in alignment with people's living experiences over a few hundred years. As discussed previously, the Punti Hakka cuisine has been passed down from the older generations and is in danger of disappearing because of the influences brought by urbanization and industrialization. Apart from the comparison of two kinds of Hakka food, I would like to introduce some of my concerns on food heritage in this chapter.

My earlier study of Hakka restaurants led me to take interest in changes taking place at different levels of production, distribution, and consumption. I examined freshwater fishpond cultivation not only as a traditional primary industry but also as a part of regional development in the context of the longer-term history and social formation of the fishing community in the Inner Deep Bay, Hong Kong. I investigated the local community's relationships with the government, developers, and environmentalists in a cultural-political context, and was able to identify their problems in maintaining the traditional practice of freshwater fish farming. In particular, I realized that freshwater fish farming did not receive enough technical support from the government, and fish farmers could only survive with a good sense of the market need. In other words, some of the costly species, such as grey mullet fed with peanut residue and mud carp, are no longer locally produced. I became concerned about resource maintenance in relation to heritage safeguarding because of these issues.

In order to enrich our understanding of foodways as intangible heritage, attention should be paid to the roles that institutions and instruments—such as state policy, institutional monitoring, communal tradition, and individual commitment—play in preserving foodways. Based on my studies on fishers of freshwater fish cultivation and the life history of local chefs, I investigate the significance and roles played by the local community and individuals in Hong Kong for safeguarding food heritage, and the following three cases are representative of the challenges faced by these agents and players in preserving intangible heritage.

## Resource as Heritage: The Ecological Role of Polyculture Freshwater Fish Farming and Related Networks

We know that some countries establish inventory lists of the varieties of crops and vegetables they used to grow in the past, and others recognize their agricultural heritage with the promotion of traditional techniques. In Hong Kong, fishery is probably the last major primary industry, and commercial freshwater fishponds are mostly located in the north-eastern part of the New Territories. The yield from these fishponds has been declining due to many factors, such as a lack of labour force, ageing of the local fishing community, pollution, and competition resulting from low-cost fish imported from mainland China. The decline of this industry reflects not only the severe loss of farming practices of polyculture as a traditional skill but also a series of related activities such as market networks, customers' relations, culinary practices, and the ecological role that supports the migratory birds' activities, which are an important part of the environmental support and post-war, socio-economic development of contemporary Hong Kong society. Therefore, when we regard freshwater fish farming as a heritage, it is a conflation of both cultural and ecological knowledge intertwined with its unique development that started in the early twentieth century (see Figure 5.1).

To improve the economic return of the fish-farming industry, during the last decade, the Agriculture, Fisheries and Conservation Department (AFCD) did try to introduce various kinds of non-local species such as tench (*Tinca tinca*), Chinese long-snout catfish, and jade perch. However, these attempts were not very successful because local customers found tench too bony, while the long-snout catfish's unpleasant look discouraged customers from buying it. As for Australian jade perch, the AFCD made several unsuccessful attempts at hatching eggs with a view to reducing the cost of imported fish fry. Finally, in 2007, the AFCD successfully produced Australian jade perch fry, and this helped local fish farmers secure a stable supply of fish fry at lower costs. However, Australian jade perch can only be engaged in monoculture because of its aggressive eating habits, while most local farmers practise polyculture in freshwater fish farming.

Instead of helping local farmers in traditional polyculture, it seems that the AFCD is more interested in introducing exotic species

**Figure 5.1:** Fish harvesting in Tai San Wai, Yuen Long, New Territories

that might not fit well with traditional systems and practices. I asked AFCD's officers why they had not developed local fry production given that there was a high demand for grey mullet fry and fingerlings, which were mostly imported from the Mainland and Taiwan, with a small proportion caught in local coastal waters. I was told by a senior government officer that such taking of fish would be regarded as an agricultural subsidy which is not allowed in member countries of the World Trade Organization (WTO). I was not convinced but that was what they had decided. Finally, when talking about foodways as intangible heritage, attention should be paid to how the resource can be produced in a sustainable fashion and should be preserved with knowledge of the local ecological system. With the idea of the Northern Metropolis development mentioned in *The Chief Executive's 2021 Policy Address*, there is no doubt that the fishpond landscape will be tremendously changed in the coming decades. We should therefore pay more attention to keeping a good balance of food heritage, conservation, and development for the well-being of the society.

## Retail Network as Heritage: Food Security Management and Relevant Knowledge

In addition to the issue of resources, retail trade networks also need to be considered in studies of the heritage preservation of foodways. Together with importation, both wholesale and retail, trading systems not only represent business activities but also local networks of long-term connections with various social sectors. One of the best-known cases is Bestor's (2004) study of *Tsukiji* in which most of the tuna consumed in the Tokyo area was auctioned and sold. Through the investigation of the trade operation, in relation to those relevant networks, it proved obvious that the trade system in *Tsukiji* formed an important institution that helped safeguard the food heritage of Japanese society. A similar issue for dried products occurred in the Hong Kong neighbourhood of Sheung Wan. This area is made up of clusters of streets full of dried marine product importers, wholesalers, retailers, and modern mini-supermarkets that sell mainly dried seafood. These traders handle dried-food commodities from all over the world, such as abalones from Japan, sea cucumbers from Indonesia, salty fish from Bangladesh, herbal medicines from mainland China, local harvested preserved shrimp paste, aged tangerine peels, fish maws, ginseng, and birds' nests among other delicacies. The trading network itself is an important system of quality as well as safety control and should be included within studies of Chinese foodways. Traditional trade systems, for instance, are not just a kind of logistic division that encourages specialization; they are also a kind of informal quality and safety control that is monitored through various levels of transactions including importers, wholesalers, retailers, and sales. In the following example, a snake meat shop illustrates the traditional and significant role that retail trade plays in preserving Cantonese food heritage in the fast-changing society of Hong Kong.

Cantonese cuisine is different from most of the Chinese regional cuisines because of its consumption of game foods such as snake, wild birds, and various hunted animals. I will use the snake retail shop as a case study to demonstrate the trade network and its relevant sociocultural meanings. First of all, snake is a reptile sometimes caught in the wild, so a snake shop needs to make sure that their snakes do not carry parasites. This is especially important for customers who come for the raw gall bladder. In addition, snake shops often provide snake meat for restaurants since snake meat is handled differently. I have had the opportunity to meet a snake meat provider, Ming, who was born in Guangzhou and came to Hong Kong in 1948 as a teenager. He works in his father's 'snake shop'. Ming told me that snake shops were commonly found in Guangzhou, Macau, and Hong Kong in the beginning of the last century, and snake soup has been very popular since the 1950s.

Snake banquets used to be important events held by various clan associations and unions in the autumn and winter seasons. In the past, people bought not only snake soup from the shop but also fresh snake meat for making soup at home. Besides snake meat, they made various products from snake gall bladders by combining them with items such as rice wine, ginger, pepper, and aged and dried tangerine peel. They are not strong medicine but are considered helpful domestic herbal drugs for minor problems in Chinese people's daily life.

Thus, this kind of retail system is complicated in the sense that it involves business relationships with wholesalers, restaurants, and even walk-in customers, as well as techniques acquired through traditional apprenticeship. As for the techniques of handling snakes for restaurants and retail, Ming recalled that 'at the beginning, learning was never easy'. He said that instead of learning about choosing and handling snakes, he was asked to wash the floor and work on other miscellaneous things for the shop. After working in the same shop for several decades, Ming has become a well-known figure among high-class Cantonese restaurants that serve snake soup mainly in autumn and early winter. Handling live poisonous snakes is never easy, and the apprenticeship system is still considered necessary for such jobs. However, as fewer young people are joining the business and there is less demand for snake meat, the industry has seen an increasing loss of traditional snake handling techniques. There is also less medicine made for the retail market.

## The Link between the Preservation of Recipes and the Establishment of Archives, Database, and the Documentation of Oral Traditions in Culinary Skills

Preserving family recipes in Hong Kong society is not a matter of filing archives but knowledge transfer between generations. Speaking from my own experience, my grandmother used to prepare different kinds of

New Year food for our own consumption and as gifts for relatives and friends. My mother still prepares some of these dishes for the Lunar New Year. However, the amount and varieties prepared are far less these days. I am not sure whether we are going to carry on with this tradition, as we can buy similar products from local shops. This situation is not only limited to local festive snacks but is also commonly reflected through the commercialization of *puhn choi* and the accessibility of homestyle cooking in restaurants (Cheung 2005). As noted earlier, the concept of *puhn choi* has been widely adopted, commercialized, and catered for families that do not want to prepare meals during festive gatherings. Apart from buying takeout *puhn choi*, rather than cooking with family recipes for special events, we can regard the accessibility of homestyle cooking both in restaurants and fast-growing dessert shops as an indicator of the decline of family cooking.

Hong Kong has more than 300,000 foreign domestic workers (mostly from the Philippines and Indonesia) in 10 to 15 per cent of Hong Kong's households, and the domestic workers do most of the cooking, using recipes not inherited within the family. I speculate that only a very few learn traditional dishes from the families they work with. Moreover, eating out is very common in Hong Kong, and family meals are frequently eaten in fast-food chains and restaurants. If people choose to eat at home, instant or convenient food packages can be purchased easily from both the wet markets and supermarkets. This makes family recipes inherited from senior family members less important. People who want homestyle dishes or desserts can find the foods easily in nearby restaurants and they do not need to pay too much. Thus, homestyle cooking and family dishes are not only available in the domestic sphere but can also be enjoyed in eateries and restaurants. One extreme case might be the emergence of the private kitchens in Hong Kong during the 1990s.

As I mentioned earlier, private kitchens represent a contemporary conflation of the everyday, homemade food with a commercialized rendition and an image of home. The personalities of the restaurant owner-hosts are well presented. The overall domestic arrangement of the interior and not using artificial substances such as MSG in their cooking—a concern of the health-conscious consumer—reinforces the image of domestic food in traditional homestyle cooking. In contrast to mainstream restaurants that have more tables and dress their staff in uniforms, private kitchens are recognized for their small size and informal atmosphere. The feel of being at home and enjoying authentic food in a private kitchen is important, as it provides comfort and a sense of belonging that most Hong Kong people appear to seek. The popularity of Hong Kong's private kitchens thus reflects not only an image of being exclusive but, most importantly, a sense of traditional homestyle cooking. This reinforces the idea of belonging—eating at home instead of at an ordinary eatery or restaurant open to any customer. The popularity of private kitchens, however, may also reflect the loss of family recipes as we move towards rapid urbanization and modernization.

The practice of preservation and heritage management represents the knowledge system instead of single-food items, and these three case studies remind us of the difficulties in deciding whether they should be considered intangible heritage and how they should be protected. It is true that these cases all share important knowledge of foodways passed down from previous generations. Yet, they have undergone transformations in their survival and have become commercialized. The case of Hong Kong's fishery industry illustrates how it has become difficult for local farmers to operate a traditional coastal polyculture system because of the decreasing market demands for certain kinds of bony freshwater fish and high labour costs. In particular, without governmental support, the traditional food production system can hardly be sustained, and these problems with local resources have consequences for food heritage. The snake shop represents a unique retail system with traditional practice playing multiple roles; however, we can make it a showcase for understanding how it safeguards important aspects of Cantonese cuisine and secures food safety through the traditional apprenticeship. In the homestyle cooking case study, family recipes are disappearing as the new generations fail to inherit the skills from their parents and grandparents, and domestic food with local recipes is prepared by the commercial sectors instead. What I would like to emphasize here is that we are losing the food that people used to eat as well as the relevant knowledge and values. At the same time, we are losing ourselves as it will be too late to regard the dishes as heritage after they have been modified commercially. Thus, the timing of recognition is the key to intangible heritage preservation, but it tends to be too late in the context of change and the alteration of tradition, or it is too early when it is still commercially sustained (Cheung 2013).

# 6
# Concluding Remarks

This book is my personal voyage as well as a food expedition in understanding Hong Kong. I hope that readers, who have had similar journeys in other countries, will find parallels because Hong Kong foodways are most likely not alone in the ways they have developed.

In my earlier research on Hong Kong foodways regarding influences from regional Cantonese food, I suggested that the popularity and subsequent decline of Hakka restaurants served as markers of Hong Kong's drastic social change and economic development from the 1950s to the late 1990s (Cheung 2001). My study of Hakka restaurants demonstrated that Hakka cuisine initially became popular because it was tasty and rich in meat protein, an important consideration for those employed in the energy-intensive industrial sector during the 1950s when Hong Kong's large-scale infrastructure flourished. I also argued that the decline of the Hakka restaurants in the 1980s was related to a dietary revolution that took place in Hong Kong due to a change in people's social values and taste, as well as in foodways in general. Hong Kong people were looking for different ways to represent their new, globally connected status; they wanted to differentiate themselves from their earlier concerns that focused primarily on the economic and nutritional value of food.

There are countless daily examples about changes in foodways during the post-war era and how traditional kinds of food have remained the same yet changed. Meanwhile, new kinds of food have been introduced and localized in contemporary Hong Kong society. Indeed, the emergence of *nouvelle* Cantonese cuisine served as an important indicator of the social construction of Hong Kong society. By the late 1970s, a visibly cosmopolitan Hong Kong with generations of Western-educated citizens was firmly in place. Parallel to this post-war transformation, the modified Cantonese cuisine reflected how Hong Kong's social values were constructed. The transformation gave rise to the *nouvelle* Cantonese cuisine in the late 1970s, which combined exotic or expensive ingredients and Western catering. Taking advantage of fast transportation, this style of cuisine was characterized by exotic ingredients, new recipes, adventurous cooking techniques, excellent catering service, and outstanding décor and ambience. *Nouvelle* Cantonese cuisine was a taste deliberately created and pursued by the local and foreign middle class. This process of culinary invention may reflect broad social and cultural trends in the late 1970s when Hong Kong's increasingly wealthy and new middle-class were attracted to a more glamorous lifestyle that stressed greater refinement.

With the incoming of various kinds of cuisines in the 1970s, Hong Kong people also became more interested in travelling abroad. South-East Asia, mainland China, Taiwan, and Japan were probably the most common destinations among the general public. However, it was probably about the same time when Hong Kong people tried not to stay with Chinese food but were willing to get the taste as well as eating experience at the place they visited. Here, I can share an episode about a friend who visited me when I was studying in Tokyo in the 1980s. This friend joined a tour from Hong Kong and visited Tokyo for a few days. He told me that most of the meals arranged by the tour company were Chinese food. Those who were interested in Japanese food such as sushi and sashimi (mainly raw sliced fish) would have to pay extra for a special meal in the evenings. The rationale behind that kind of arrangement was because the majority of Hong Kong people were not familiar with Japanese food (especially raw fish, which is not common in the Chinese diet). However, some tour members might want to try while travelling in Japan. From this shared personal experience, I suggest that Hong Kong people have been changing, but the conventional practices will not disappear overnight, and the new diet has been introduced in alignment of the society's development and interactions with the outside world.

Hong Kong has become economically advanced and culturally international since the late 1970s; individuals have sought to identify themselves with society by varying means. By looking at food and cuisine as a cultural marker of the identity and status of people, international cuisine in restaurants serves to identify a means for people to compete as equals in the international arena. However, food consumed at home is by far more traditional and conservative, with concerns for safety, health, traditional hot/cold balance, and ritual taboos. A boundary is maintained and well defined between eating at home and outside. Nevertheless, this negotiation between traditionalism and globalism in relation to domestic issues can be wholly observed in Hong Kong. Furthermore, the ingredients used are highly similar in most families, and cooking styles seldom vary. For example, boiled soup, steamed fish, fried seasonal green vegetables with small pieces of meat, and bean curd are all typical family dishes, and rice is almost always the staple food in Hong Kong homes. The difference between eating habits inside and outside the home is a telling one and reflects the dichotomy of Hong Kong itself. Hong Kong is a cosmopolitan city boasting international sophistication on the one hand, while on the other hand, it is an extension of Chinese culture with long-standing Cantonese traditions. Looking for nostalgia and the homemade became popular in the early 1990s, and the related cultural and political influences should not be overlooked. I hope the popularization of *puhn choi* and private kitchens brought insights into the societal changes; in particular, *puhn choi* is not only a kind of nostalgic food in the postcolonial context but also a dish that demonstrates the significance of commensality in Hong Kong society. In other words, from the practice of *puhn choi* consumption both in family festive gatherings (做節) and social networking events, we can understand the importance of eating together among families and friends. This practice can justify the phenomenon of 'mobile phones eat first' (手機先食, meaning that we take pictures of our food before we eat it) and can be explained as a kind of media-oriented commensality. Again, with the recent increased interest in local Hakka dishes, homemade dumplings, and snacks among Hong Kong people, I would say that it is well on its way to becoming a new trend towards the demand of local traditions in the context of cultural engagement in countryside conservation.

Another area that I have not covered, albeit a significant one, is the use of food in media and communication. Modern mass media can influence consumption habits; for example, advertisements and TV programmes give guidelines for or teach people how to choose and purchase goods and services. The mass media bombards the public with all sorts of images via advertisements in television, newspapers, magazines, mail, the internet, radio broadcasts, and posters on the subways. If we look at the development of Hong Kong television cooking shows during the last several decades, we can easily divide them into three phases. In the first phase, cooking was demonstrated as evidence of competent domestic skills for women. Such presentations were usually performed by an elegant woman who advised on what to cook on particular days and shared her personal experiences about how to keep everyone in the family healthy by serving traditional Cantonese simmered soups and fresh seasonal dishes. This kind of cooking show can still be found in afternoon programming as part of various housekeeping series; books and video CDs are also available on this topic. The second phase emerged with the rapid increase in Hong Kong's living standards in which overseas travel, luxurious lifestyle, and gourmet dining were enjoyed by a rising middle class that was eager to express social status. This is especially the case with the consumption of expensive food introduced by pop stars, celebrities, and food writers in many of Hong Kong's televised travel programmes. Celebrities introduced local cuisines and famous eateries in particular tourist destinations. They also explained how local people prepared and cooked the dishes they ate and some exotic ingredients and other aspects of the dishes were introduced. The third phase combines cooking skills and competitions with a focus on teamwork, family ties, and individual achievements, among other qualities. Instead of luxurious ingredients and professional culinary techniques, many of these TV and social media cooking programmes emphasize more of the emotional attachments, personal narratives, and health concerns, hailing back to how food is related to their experiences and challenges. Again, the narratives which are shown in the third phase have also been widely used in films and TV dramas, and some of those food statements have even been seriously taken by the mass public.

Nowadays, it is no doubt that the number of vegans and vegetarians has increased substantially in Hong Kong. Also, there have been more young people showing an interest in agriculture and organic farming. These phenomena remind us that food cannot be understood merely in the context of nutrition, religion, and economics; we must also consider how people project eating as a kind of ideal lifestyle they are looking for. After the social movements of 2019, there was a new genre of eateries called 'yellow shops' that attracted customers who had certain kinds of political stands related to the movement, even though the boundary was sometimes not clear. Another recent change due to the COVID-19 pandemic was food delivery and development of food banks in some old neighbourhoods.

To conclude, this is a monograph of my studies on Hong Kong foodways in the last two decades. It elucidates my research findings on a range of issues, including post-war migrants, agricultural practices, globalization, heritage, and conservation. My anthropological studies of foodways suggest that this topic is not only about culinary skills and nutritional values but more importantly, it is also about the cultural meanings and social significance of what Hong Kong people ate in the past century. Having said that, I hope this book will be considered more than a review of Hong Kong foodways and that it could indicate a direction towards a holistic understanding of foodways and Hong Kong society.

# Notes

## Chapter 1

1. As a local oyster farmer relayed: 'Legend has it that a ship full of ceramics was stranded on a sandbar in the storm during the Dragon Boat Festival. To save the ship, the crew reluctantly threw the porcelains and potteries overboard. A few years later, a boat was stranded on the very same sandbar. When people got into the water and tried to push the boat, they discovered something strange on the seabed—oysters attached to and grew on the ceramics. That was how people here discovered oysters and got to know how to rear them in a massive scale' (quoted from Lee and Cheung 2017, 17).

2. Mow is Cantonese for mu in Mandarin. One mu is equal to 0.0667 hectare or 0.1667 acre.

3. Lin's calculation was based on 1 mow = 0.2 acre; however, the more accurate scale should be 1 mow = 0.1667 acre.

## Chapter 2

1. Plastic and garment manufacturing industries grew from the late 1950s until the early 1980s. After the light industry development, Hong Kong changed to focus on finance and banking until nowadays.

2. This was the only one still in business in 2021.

3. There are some common dishes in the appetizers such as cold noodles and

shredded chicken with sesame sauce, chopped vegetables with dried tofu, marinated wheat gluten with black fungus, pickled turnips with soy sauce, veggie duck (tofu skin), fried yellow croaker, and smoked grass carp.

## Chapter 3

1. They might not have a Chinese name at that time.
2. The history of Benihana (紅花) and its founder, Mr Rocky Aoki, can be found at https://www.benihana.com/about/history/.

## Chapter 4

1. For more on the handover in 1997, see Abbas (1997); Skeldon (1994).

# Works Cited

Abbas, Ackbas. 1997. *Hong Kong: Culture and the Politics of Disappearance*. Hong Kong: Hong Kong University Press.

Akamine, Jun. 2021. 'Tastes for Blubber: Diversity and Locality of Whale Meat Foodways in Japan'. *Asian Education and Development Studies* 10, no. 1: 105–114.

Anderson, Eugene. 1988. *The Food of China*. New Haven, CT: Yale University Press.

Anderson, Jay. 1971. 'A Solid Sufficiency: An Ethnography of Yeoman Foodways in Stuart England'. Unpublished PhD dissertation, University of Pennsylvania.

Appadurai, Arjun. 1988. 'How to Make a National Cuisine: Cookbooks in Contemporary India'. *Comparative Study of Society and History* 30, no. 1: 3–24.

Bestor, Theodore C. 2004. *Tsukiji: The Fish Market at the Center of the World*. Berkeley: University of California Press.

Chan, Kwok Shing. 2011. 'Traditionality and Hybridity: A Village Cuisine in Metropolitan Hong Kong'. *Visual Anthropology* 24, no. 1: 171–188.

Chan, May. 2003a. 'Top Food Guide's Flavour of the Mouth'. *South China Morning Post*, 3 March 2003.

Chan, May. 2003b. 'Illegal Eateries Want Licence-Free Status'. *South China Morning Post*, 3 March 2003.

Chan, Selina C. 2010. 'Food, Memories, and Identities in Hong Kong'. *Identities* 17: 204–227.

Chan, Selina C. 2019. 'Tea Cafés and the Hong Kong Identity: Food Culture and Hybridity'. *China Information: A Journal on Contemporary China Studies* 33, no. 3: 311–328.

Cheng, Sea Ling. 1997. 'Back to the Future: Herbal Tea Shops in Hong Kong'. In *Hong Kong: The Anthropology of a Chinese Metropolis*, edited by Grant Evans and Maria Siumi Tam, 51–73. Surrey and Honolulu: Curzon and University of Hawai'i Press.

Cheung, Sidney C. H. 1996. 'Change of Ainu Images in Japan: A Reflexive Study of Pre-war and Post-war Photo-Images of Ainu'. *Visual Anthropology* 9, no. 1: 1–24.

Cheung, Sidney C. H. 1999. 'The Meanings of a Heritage Trail in Hong Kong'. *Annals of Tourism Research* 26, no. 3: 570–588.

Cheung, Sidney C. H. 2000a. 'Men, Women, and "Japanese" as Outsiders: A Case Study of Postcards with Ainu Images'. *Visual Anthropology* 13, no. 3: 227–255.

Cheung, Sidney C. H. 2000b. 'Martyrs, Mystery, and Memory behind a Communal Hall'. *Traditional Dwellings and Settlements Review* 11, no. 2: 29–39.

Cheung, Sidney C. H. 2001. 'Hakka Restaurants: A Study of the Consumption of Food in Post-war Hong Kong Society'. In *Changing Chinese Foodways in Asia*, edited by David Wu and Tan Chee Beng, 81–95. Hong Kong: The Chinese University of Hong Kong Press.

Cheung, Sidney C. H. 2003. 'Remembering through Space: The Politics of Heritage in Hong Kong'. *International Journal of Heritage Studies* 9, no. 1: 7–26.

Cheung, Sidney C. H. 2004. 'Japanese Anthropology and Depictions of the Ainu'. In *The Making of Anthropology in East and Southeast Asia*, edited by Shinji Yamashita, Joseph Bosco, and J. S. Eades, 136–151. Oxford and New York: Berghahn Books.

Cheung, Sidney C. H. 2005. 'Consuming "Low" Cuisine after Hong Kong's Handover: Village Banquets and Private Kitchen'. *Asian Studies Review* 29, no. 3: 259–273.

Cheung, Sidney C. H. 2007. 'Fish in the Marsh: A Case Study of Freshwater Fish Farming in Hong Kong'. In *Food and Foodways in Asia: Resource, Tradition, and Cooking*, edited by Sidney C. H. Cheung and Tan Chee-Beng, 37–50. London and New York: Routledge Press.

Cheung, Sidney C. H. 2008. 'Wetland Tourism in Hong Kong: From Birdwatcher to Mass Ecotourist'. In *Asian Tourism: Growth and Change*, edited by Janet Cochrane, 259–267. London: Elsevier Science.

Cheung, Sidney C. H. 2011. 'The Politics of Wetlandscape: Fishery Heritage and Natural Conservation in Hong Kong'. *International Journal of Heritage Studies* 17, no. 1: 36–45.

Cheung, Sidney C. H. 2013. 'From Foodways to Intangible Heritage: A Case Study of Chinese Culinary Resource, Retail and Recipe in Hong Kong'. *International Journal of Heritage Studies* 19, no. 4: 353–364.

Cheung, Sidney C. H. 2015a. 'The Social Life of American Crayfish in Asia'. In *Re-orienting Cuisine: East Asian Foodways in the Twenty-First Century*, edited by Kwang Ok Kim, 221–237. New York and Oxford: Berghahn Books.

Cheung, Sidney C. H. 2015b. 'From Cajun Crayfish to Spicy Little Lobster: A Tale of Local Culinary Politics in a Third-Tier City in China'. In *Globalization and Asian Cuisines: Transnational Networks and Contact Zones*, edited by James Farrer, 209–228. New York: Palgrave MacMillan.

Cheung, Sidney C. H. 2017. 'New Orleans, New Territories'. In *Hong Kong Culture and Society in the New Millennium: Hong Kong as Method*, edited by Stephen Chu Yiu Wai, 79–90. New York: Springer Nature.

Cheung, Sidney C. H. 2019. 'Floating Mountain in Pearl River: A Study of Oyster Cultivation and Food Heritage in Hong Kong'. *Asian Education and Development Studies* 8, no. 4: 433–442.

Cheung, Sidney C. H. 2020. 'Reflections on the Historical Construction of Huaiyang Cuisine: A Study on the Social Development of Shanghai Foodways in Hong Kong'. *Global Food History* 6, no. 2: 128–142.

Cheung, Sidney C. H., and Tan Chee Beng, eds. 2007. *Food and Foodways in Asia: Resource, Tradition and Cooking*. London and New York: Routledge.

Cwiertka, Katarzyna, and Boudewijn Walraven, eds. 2000. *Asian Food: The Global and the Local*. Richmond, Surrey: Curzon.

Da Silva, Armando. 1977. 'Native Management of Coastal Wetlands in Hong Kong: A Case Study of Wetland Change at Tin Shui Wai Agricultural Lot,

New Territories'. Unpublished PhD dissertation, University of Hawai'i.

DeWolf, Christopher. 2017. 'Russian Hong Kong: Why Do Hong Kong Restaurants Serve Borscht?' *Zolima City Mag*, 4 October 2017. https://zolimacitymag.com/.

Douglas, Mary. 1966. *Purity and Danger: An Analysis of the Concepts of Pollution and Taboo*. London and New York: ARK.

Duruz, Jean. 2001. 'Home Cooking, Nostalgia, and the Purchase of Tradition'. *Traditional Dwellings and Settlements Review* 12, no. 2: 21–32.

Fung, Chi Ming. 1996. *Yuen Long Historical Relics and Monuments*, Hong Kong: Yuen Long District Board.

Fung, Emily W. Y. 1963. 'Pond Fish Culture in the New Territories of Hong Kong'. Unpublished BA thesis, University of Hong Kong.

Goody, Jack. 1982. *Cooking, Cuisine and Class: A Study in Comparative Sociology*. Cambridge: Cambridge University Press.

Grant, C. J. 1971. 'Fish Farming in Hong Kong'. In *The Changing Face of Hong Kong*, edited by D. J. Dwyer, 36–46. Hong Kong: Hong Kong Branch of the Royal Asiatic Society.

Guldin, Gregory E. 1977. '"Little Fujian (Fukien)": Sub-neighborhood and Community in North Point, Hong Kong'. *Journal of the Hong Kong Branch of the Royal Asiatic Society* 17: 112–129.

Guldin, Gregory E. 1979. '"Overseas" at Home: The Fujianese of Hong Kong'. Ann Arbor, MI: University Microfilms International.

Guo, Peiyuan (郭培源), and Cheng Jian (程建). 2006. *Legends of Shajing Oyster in Thousand Years* (千年傳奇沙井蠔). Beijing (北京): Haichao Press (海潮出版社).

Handler, Richard. 1986. 'Authenticity'. *Anthropology Today* 2, no. 1: 2–4.

Harris, Marvin. 1986. *Good to Eat: Riddles of Food and Culture*. London: Allen and Unwin.

Ho, Hao-Tzu. 2020. 'Cosmopolitan Locavorism: Global Local-Food Movements in Postcolonial Hong Kong'. *Food, Culture & Society* 23, no. 2: 137–154.

Hong Kong Special Administrative Region Government [HKSARG]. 2005a. 'Safety Tips for Enjoying "*Poon Choi*"'. *Government Press Release*, 15 January 2005.

# Works Cited

Hong Kong Special Administrative Region Government [HKSARG]. 2005b. 'Eat Safety during Lunar New Year'. *Government Press Release*, 5 February 2005.

Johnson, Elizabeth L., and Graham E. Johnson. 2019. *A Chinese Melting Pot: Original People and Immigrants in Hong Kong's First 'New Town'*. Hong Kong: Hong Kong University Press.

Kerner, Susanne, Cynthia Chou, and Morten Warmind. 2015. *Commensality: From Everyday Food to Feast*. London and New York: Bloomsbury Academic.

King, Michelle, ed. 2019. *Culinary Nationalism in Asia*. London: Bloomsbury Academic.

Klein, Jakob. 2007. 'Redefining Cantonese Cuisine in Post-Mao Guangzhou'. *Bulletin of the School of Oriental and African Studies* 70, no. 3: 511–537.

Lai, L. W. C., and Lam K. K. H. 1999. 'The Evolution and Future of Pond and Marine Fish Culture in Hong Kong'. *Aquaculture Economics & Management* 3, no. 3: 254–266.

Lau, Siu-kai, and Kuan Hsin-chi. 1988. *The Ethos of the Hong Kong Chinese*. Hong Kong: The Chinese University of Hong Kong Press.

Lee, Miriam, and Sidney C. H. Cheung. 2017. 'The World Is Your Oyster'. *Hong Kong Discovery* 98: 14–43.

Lee, Wai Yee. 1997. 'Food and Ethnicity: A Study of Eating Habits among Chiu Chow People in Hong Kong (in Chinese)'. Unpublished MPhil thesis, the Chinese University of Hong Kong.

Leitch, Alison. 2003. 'Slow Food and the Politics of Pork Fat: Italian Food and European Identity'. *Ethnos* 68, no. 4: 427–462.

Lévi-Strauss, Claude. 1969. *The Raw and the Cooked*. Translated by John and Doreen Weightman. New York: Harper and Row.

Lin, S. Y. 1940. 'Fish Culture in Ponds in the New Territories of Hong Kong'. *Journal of the Hong Kong Fisheries Research Station* 1: 161–193.

Liu, Haiming. 2015. *From Canton Restaurant to Panda Express: A History of Chinese Food in the United States*. New Brunswick, NJ: Rutgers University Press.

Lum, Casey M. K. 2013. 'Understanding Urban Foodways and Communicative Cities: A Taste of Hong Kong's Yumcha Culture as Urban Communication'.

In *The Urban Communication Reader III: Communicative Cities and Urban Communication in the 21st Century*, edited by Susan Drucker, Victoria Gallenger, and Matthew Matsaganis, 53–76. New York: Peter Lang.

Ma, Eric Kit-wai. 1999. *Culture, Politics and Television in Hong Kong*. London and New York: Routledge.

Martin, Diana. 2001. 'Food Restrictions in Pregnancy among Hong Kong Mothers'. In *Changing Chinese Foodways in Asia*, edited by David Wu and Tan Chee Beng, 97–122. Hong Kong: The Chinese University of Hong Kong Press.

Mintz, Sidney W. 1985. *Sweetness and Power: The Place of Sugar in Modern History*. New York: Viking Penguin.

Mintz, Sidney W. 1996.*Tasting Food, Tasting Freedom: Excursions into Eating, Culture, and the Past*. Boston: Beacon.

Mintz, Sidney W., and Christine M. Du Bois. 2002. 'The Anthropology of Food and Eating'. *Annual Review of Anthropology* 30: 99–119.

Morton, Brian, and P. S. Wong. 1975. 'The Pacific Oyster Industry in Hong Kong'. *Journal of the Royal Asiatic Society Hong Kong Branch* 15: 139–149.

Ng, Benjamin Wai-ming. 2006. 'Imagining and Consuming Japanese Food in Hong Kong, SAR, China: A Study of Culinary Domestication and Hybridization'. *Asian Profile* 34, no. 4: 299–308.

Ohnuki-Tierney, Emiko. 1993. *Rice as Self: Japanese Identities through Time*. Princeton: Princeton University Press.

Potter, Jack M. 1968. *Capitalism and the Chinese Peasant: Social and Economic Change in a Hong Kong Village*. Oakland: University of California Press.

Sahlins, Marshall D. 1976. *Culture and Practical Reason*. Chicago: University of Chicago Press.

Simonds, Nina. 2004. 'In Hong Kong, Home Kitchens with Open Doors'. *The New York Times*, 15 August 2004.

Simoons, Frederick. 1991. *Food in China: A Cultural and Historical Inquiry*. Boca Raton: CRC Press.

Skeldon, Ronald, ed. 1994. *Reluctant Exiles? Migration from Hong Kong and the New Overseas Chinese*. Hong Kong: Hong Kong University Press.

Sterling, Richard, Elizabeth Chong, and Lushan Charles Qin. 2001. *World Food Hong Kong*. Victoria, Australia: Lonely Planet.

Suen, C. S. 1955. 'Fish Ponds in Un Long'. Unpublished thesis, University of Hong Kong.

Sutton, David E. 2001. *Remembrance of Repasts: An Anthropology of Food and Memory*. Oxford and New York: Berg.

Tambiah, Stanley J. 1969. 'Animals Are Good to Think and Good to Prohibit'. *Ethnology* 8, no. 4: 423–459.

Tang, Kwan Chi. 2002. 'A Big Bowl Feast'. In *Tell Your Hong Kong Story*, edited by the Hong Kong Tourism Board, 4–5. Hong Kong: Hong Kong Tourism Board.

Tobin, Joseph J., ed. 1992. *Re-made in Japan: Everyday Life and Consumer Taste in a Changing Society*. New Haven, CT: Yale University Press.

UNESCO. 2003. *Convention for the Safeguarding of the Intangible Cultural Heritage*. Paris: UNESCO.

Wang, Caroline Yiqian. 2021. 'Hong Kong Identities through Food: Tracing Developments and Variations of Pineapple Buns in Modern Complexities'. *Food, Culture & Society*. https://doi.org/10.1080/15528014.2021.1932274.

Watson, James L. 1987. 'From the Common Pot: Feasting with Equals in Chinese Society'. *Anthropos* 82: 389–401.

Watson, James L., ed. 1997. *Golden Arches East: McDonald's in East Asia*. Stanford: Stanford University Press.

Watson, James L., and Melissa L. Caldwell, eds. 2005. *The Cultural Politics of Food and Eating: A Reader*. Malden: Blackwell.

Wilk, Richard R., ed. 2006a. *Fast Food/Slow Food: The Cultural Economy of the Global Food System*. Lanham, MD: Altamira Press.

Wilk, Richard R. 2006b. *Home Cooking in the Global Village: Caribbean Food from Buccaneers to Ecotourists*. Oxford and New York: Berg.

Wills, John E. Jr. 2011. *China and Maritime Europe, 1500–1800: Trade, Settlement, Diplomacy, and Mission*. Cambridge: Cambridge University Press.

Wu, David Y. H. 2001. 'Chinese Café in Hong Kong'. In *Changing Chinese Foodways in Asia*, edited by David Wu and Tan Chee Beng, 71–80. Hong Kong: The Chinese University of Hong Kong Press.

Works Cited

Wu, David Y. H., and Sidney C. H. Cheung, eds. 2002. *The Globalization of Chinese Food*. Surrey: RoutledgeCurzon.

Wu, David Y. H., and Tan Chee Beng, eds. 2001. *Changing Chinese Foodways in Asia*. Hong Kong: The Chinese University of Hong Kong Press.

Yeung, W. W. H. 1968. 'Pond-Fish Culture in Brackish Water Ponds of Deep Bay Area with Nam Shan Wai as an Example'. Unpublished BA thesis, University of Hong Kong.